NOOK® HD

FOR

DUMMIES®

PORTABLE EDITION

NOOK® HD

FOR

DUMMIES®

PORTABLE EDITION

by Corey Sandler

WILEY

John Wiley & Sons, Inc.

NOOK® HD For Dummies®, Portable Edition

Published by
John Wiley & Sons, Inc.
111 River Street
Hoboken, NJ 07030-5774
www.wiley.com

WILEY

About the Author

Corey Sandler is a voracious reader and indefatigable author: books, magazine pieces and, ages ago, newspapers. He has written more than 200 books at last count, about computers and technology, history, sports, and business. When he's not at the keyboard, Sandler travels all over the world as a destination lecturer aboard luxury cruise ships. (Someone has to do it.)

Okay, so sometimes he is fatigable. That happens when you carry 150 pounds of luggage including a laptop, two tablets, three cameras, four lenses, five electrical plugs, half a dozen books to read and consult, and a hogshead of lecture notes printed out and neatly bound to sit on a lectern. And that's one major reason why he's a fan of electronic books. It's good for his back.

Sandler studied journalism at Syracuse University; he also took some courses to learn how to program a gigantic IBM mainframe computer and worked nights at a newspaper printing plant.

He began his career as a daily newspaper reporter in Ohio and then New York, moving on to a post as a correspondent for Associated Press. From there he joined Ziff-Davis Publishing as the first executive editor of *PC Magazine*. He wrote his first book about computers in 1983 and hasn't come close to stopping. When he's not out to sea or in a foreign country and living on his smartphone, tablet, and computer, he's at home on Nantucket Island 30 miles off the coast of Massachusetts. He shares his life with his wife Janice; two grown children have their own careers elsewhere on the continent.

You can see Sandler's current list of books on his website at www.sandlerbooks.com, and send an email through the links you find there. He promises to respond to courteous inquiries as quickly as he can. Spam, on the other hand, will receive the death penalty.

Dedication

This book is once again dedicated to my home team. Janice has put up with me for more than 30 years and still laughs at most of my jokes. My children, William and Tessa, are no longer constantly underfoot; they have embarked now on careers of their own, but when I need consultation on social networks and cultural references beyond the scope of Old Dad, they're the first to text, IM, or tweet.

Author's Acknowledgments

This book bears just one name on the cover, but that's only part of the story.

Thanks to the smart and capable crew at Wiley, including Katie Mohr and the rest of the editorial and production staff, who turned the taps of my keyboard into the book you hold in the electronic device in the palm of your hand.

Also, my appreciation to long-time publishing collaborator Tonya Maddox Cupp, who once again managed the process with grace and humor.

And as always, thanks to you for buying this book. Go forth and enjoy your NOOK HD or HD+ tablet for escapades on the World Wide Web, audio, video, games, and easy (and weightless) access to millions of great works of literature, thoughtful history, and analysis.

As the great Harvard man Charles William Eliot once wrote, "Books are the quietest and most constant of friends; they are the most accessible and wisest of counselors, and the most patient of teachers."

Publisher's Acknowledgments

We're proud of this book; please send us your comments at http://dummies. custhelp.com. For other comments, please contact our Customer Care Department within the U.S. at 877-762-2974, outside the U.S. at 317-572-3993, or fax 317-572-4002.

Some of the people who helped bring this book to market include the following:

Acquisitions and Editorial

Project Editor: Tonya Maddox Cupp

Senior Acquisitions Editor: Katie Mohr

Editorial Manager: Jodi Jensen

Editorial Assistant: Annie Sullivan

Sr. Editorial Assistant: Cherie Case

Cover Photo: © Evgeny Terentev / iStockphoto (background image) / Nook HD and Nook HD+ images courtesy of Barnes & Noble

Composition Services

Project Coordinator: Patrick Redmond

Layout and Graphics: Andrea Hornberger

Proofreaders: John Greenough, Wordsmith Editorial

Indexer: Steve Rath

Publishing and Editorial for Technology Dummies

Richard Swadley, Vice President and Executive Group Publisher

Andy Cummings, Vice President and Publisher

Mary Bednarek, Executive Acquisitions Director

Mary C. Corder, Editorial Director

Publishing for Consumer Dummies

Kathleen Nebenhaus, Vice President and Executive Publisher

Composition Services

Debbie Stailey, Director of Composition Services

Contents at a Glance

Introduction.. 1

Chapter 1: Viewing in HD and HD+.. 5
Chapter 2: Going Home on the NOOK....................................... 23
Chapter 3: Setting Things Up 47
Chapter 4: Mastering the Reading Tools 77
Chapter 5: Stocking Shelves and Adding Apps............................. 119
Chapter 6: Going Wireless and Out on the Web............................ 161
Chapter 7: Ten-Plus Tips and Tricks..................................... 193

Index.. 211

Contents

Introduction 1

Foolish Assumptions 3
Icons Used in This Book 4
Where to Go from Here 4

Chapter 1: Viewing in HD and HD+ 5

Telling HD from HD+ 6
Inspecting the Gadget 6
The front 8
About the color touchscreen 9
Home button: ∩ 10
About the NOOK notch 10
The top side 10
The bottom 11
The left 12
The right 13
The back 13
Getting More on a microSD Card 15
Installing a microSD card 17
Formatting an SD card 19
Babying the Battery 20
Getting power from the wall 21
Locking or unlocking the tablet 22

Chapter 2: Going Home on the NOOK 23

Seeing the Parts of the Whole 23
Using the Home Screen 24
Home screen desktop 25
The nav buttons 25
Library 26
Apps 28
Web 28
Email 28
Shop 28
The shortcuts menu 28
Your NOOK Today 29

Changing Your Home Screen 30
  Removing an item from the Active Shelf 31
  Adding an item from shortcuts to the
    Home screen 31
  Removing an item from the Home screen 32
Checking Your Status Bar 32
  Left 33
  Center 33
  Right 34
Seeing What's Stocked in the System Bar 35
  Home screen 35
  Library 36
  Shop 37
Returning to Recent Reads 38
  Recent Drawer 38
  Recent Read 38
Keeping Your Gestures Polite 39
  Tap 39
  Double-tap 40
  Press and hold 40
  Swipe 41
  Scroll 42
  Drag 43
  Lift 43
  Pinch 43
  Press 44
Using the Virtual Keyboard 44

Chapter 3: Setting Things Up 47

Styling and Profiling 47
  The primary profile 48
  An adult profile 48
  A child profile 50
  Changing or deleting profiles 53
Setting Up Your NOOK the Way You Like 53
  The Quick Settings panel 54
    Home Settings 54
    Brightness 55
    Wi-Fi 55
    Airplane Mode 55
    Lock Rotation 55
    All Settings 55
  All settings 55
    Wireless & Bluetooth 55
    General 56

Application settings 59
        Home settings 60
        Email settings 62
        Calendar settings 63
        Contacts settings 64
        Browser settings 65
        Magazine/Catalog/Comics reader 66
        Shop 67
        Social accounts and NOOK Friends 68
        Reader 69
        Search 70
        NOOK Video 71
    Account settings 71
        UltraViolet 71
        Adobe Digital Editions 72
    Storage Management 72
    Device Information 73

Chapter 4: Mastering the Reading Tools. 77
    Turning Pages in Books, Magazines, and Newspapers 78
        Opening an e-book 79
        Turning the pages 80
        Understanding page numbering 80
        Moving rapidly from place to place 81
            Slip, sliding along 81
            Go to Page 82
        Mastering advanced e-book navigation 83
    Finding More Reading Tools 86
        Highlight 87
        Add Note 88
        Share Quote 90
        Look Up 91
        Find in Book 92
    The Advanced Course in Bookmarks 93
        Bookmark the page you're reading 93
        See all the bookmarks in a book 93
        Clear all bookmarks in a book 94
    Clipping Pages for a Scrapbook 94
        Saving a page in a scrapbook 95
        Viewing a scrapbook 96
        Adding a note to a scrapbook page 96
        Seeing notes attached to scrapbook pages 96
        Moving through your scrapbook 97
        Removing a page from a scrapbook 97

Designing Your Own Book 97
        Size 98
        Line Spacing 98
        Margins 99
        Font 99
        Themes 99
        Publisher Defaults 100
    Reading a Magazine 100
        Page view 101
        Article view 102
    Reading a Newspaper 102
    Reading for Kids of All Ages 103
        Moving from page to page 104
        Skipping part of a children's book 104
        Choosing a reading style 105
            Read by Myself 105
            Read to Me or Read and Play 105
            Read and Record 106
    Studying a NOOK Comics Book 107
    Flipping Through Catalogs 108
    Knowing Your PDF from Your EPUB 108
        EPUB 109
        PDF 109
    Side Loading Files 110
        Moving files from a computer to your NOOK 113
        Preparing files for the NOOK 114
        Knowing what file types work 115
        Ejecting the NOOK from a computer 116
            Windows-based computer or laptop 116
            Macintosh computer or laptop 117
    Traveling Abroad with a NOOK 118

Chapter 5: Stocking Shelves and Adding Apps 119

    Welcome B&N Shoppers! 120
    Locking Things Down 122
    Shopping from Your NOOK 124
        Searching for a specific book 127
        Buying a book 129
        Buying magazines or newspapers 130
            Buying a single issue 130
            Subscribing to a periodical 132
        Subscribing to catalogs 132
        Paying the bill 133
        Buying apps from B&N 134

Making a WishList 137
    Adding to your WishList 138
    Checking your WishList 139
    Starting a Wishlist on the B&N website 139
    Archiving to the NOOK Cloud 140
        Moving an item to the NOOK Cloud 141
        Getting back an item from the
            NOOK Cloud 141
        Looking at your NOOK Cloud storage 141
    Performing a sync or refresh 143
Lending and Borrowing Books 144
    Lending a book to NOOK Friends 145
    Lending a book of NOOK Friends 146
    Borrowing a book 148
    Setting Library privacy 149
Managing Your Library 150
    Building your own shelves 151
    Creating a shelf 151
    Adding items to a shelf 152
Going Elsewhere to Buy or Borrow 152
    About Adobe Digital Editions 152
        Preparing to use a NOOK with Adobe
            Digital Editions 153
        Installing book files using Adobe
            Digital Editions 153
    Diving into Overdrive 154
    Using Google Play Bookstore 155
        Reading a public domain book via
            Google e-bookstore 156
        Buying on Google e-bookstore 157
    Getting something for nothing 158
    Loading the right Calibre 159

Chapter 6: Going Wireless and Out on the Web 161

Working without a Wire 162
    Using the web browser 163
    Advanced browser functions 166
    Adjusting the web browser's hair 168
    Configuring web privacy and security 169
        Critical privacy and security options 171
        Cookies 171
        Form data 172
        Web security options 172
    Advanced web page settings 172

Sending and Getting Email..174
  Using the Email app...175
  Setting up an account manually.................................177
  Sending an email...179
  Replying to or forwarding a message........................181
  Deleting email..181
  Getting attached 182
  Feeling Bluetooth? 182
App-lying Yourself 183
  The supplied apps 184
  Music player..186
    Moving audio files onto the NOOK 186
    Playing an audio file from the Library 187
    Music Player modes 187
Video Playing On...188
  Subscribing to Hulu Plus...189
  Subscribing to Netflix..189
  Amazon Prime Video...190
  NOOK Video: A work in progress 190
  You and YouTube..191

Chapter 7: Ten-Plus Tips and Tricks 193

Making a Screen Capture 194
Reenergizing a Dead NOOK 196
  Not enough battery power 197
  Your recharger isn't getting juice..............................198
Keeping a NOOK Tablet Happy..199
Piloting Your NOOK at 33,000 Feet 199
Rubbing Your Prints off the Touchscreen........................200
Improving Your NOOK Warranty..201
Resetting Your NOOK...202
  Soft reset...202
  Hard reset (Deregister)..202
Fixing Wireless Weirdness 203
  I see a wireless network but can't get a
    good connection 204
  I see the network but I can't connect to it...............205
Updating the NOOK Operating System 205
Don't Pay Twice, It's All Right..206
Appy NOOK Day..206
Getting to the Root of It 207
  Getting to the root 208
  Running a second operating system..........................209
Flashing Your NOOK..209

Index...*211*

Introduction

*W*hat *is* a NOOK HD or NOOK HD+?

Depending upon how you look at it, it's one of these:

- An e-book e-reader that adds many (but not all) of the features of a tablet computer, including a wireless Internet connection and an audio and video player.
- A tablet computer (slightly less capable than some significantly more expensive competitors) with a new and improved bright, colorful touchscreen that you can use to read e-books.

It's a NOOK, which is the brand name for a line of electronic devices developed by and marketed by Barnes & Noble. Why NOOK? Why not? It's a reasonably clever name. And it is HD, as in high definition. Which brings us into uncharted territory, because there is no industry-standard definition for HD except to say that it means sharper (higher resolution) images than standard definition.

An old television set in the United States used to put out a paltry 480 horizontal lines of 720 dots. Just for the record, the NOOK HD offers 900 lines by 1,440 dots. And the NOOK HD+ defines its own territory at 1,280 lines by 1,920 dots. (If you're comparing, the NOOK HD has higher resolution than the pricier Apple iPad Mini and the NOOK HD+ is just a tad below the resolution of the fourth-generation Apple iPad itself.) If this technical stuff makes your eyes water, here's the bottom line: The more lines and dots per square inch, the more you're going to say "Wow!"

Let me begin by saluting the exemplary specifications of the NOOK HD and its larger and even-more-splendiferous cousin, the NOOK HD+. In a small and highly portable plastic case, you'll find the following:

- ✔ A high-resolution backlit LCD screen, capable of displaying crisp text in a book, magazine, a newspaper, or other document. A few minutes into reading the latest bestseller or a classic of literature you just might completely forget that there's no ink or paper involved.

- ✔ Spectacular color graphics, perfect for reading magazines, comics, or children's books. Just as an example, if you love *National Geographic* or *Sports Illustrated* or *Vanity Fair* in their print editions, you'll be blown away with their electronic versions.

- ✔ Built into the screen: the ability to sense your touch. When you need a keyboard, one appears. You can also swipe, flick, pinch, and otherwise rule your domain by hand.

- ✔ An e-reader for documents created on computers, including word processors, Excel spreadsheets, and basic PowerPoint presentations. It can read PDF files.

- ✔ A Wi-Fi radio system that connects the NOOK to the Internet.

- ✔ Bluetooth wireless communication that you can connect to tiny headsets to play music and sound, with the as-yet unconfirmed possibility of other devices like keyboards and video routers.

- ✔ A full-featured browser allows you to visit any page on the web and shop for shoes, read the news, get the blues, and just about whatever else you do in cyberspace. The Internet connection flows both ways: You can buy e-books and magazines and you can put aside the e-book to do a bit of research on your own.

- ✔ You can download individual copies or get a free subscription to any of a number of catalogs. You can drool over that gorgeous dress or that handsome sport coat or that spectacular fruitcake, and then go to the web or a telephone to place your order.

- ✔ Built-in facilities to read and write email using nearly all major email providers.

- ✔ Electronic piping that streams videos: Barnes & Noble offers its own selection of movies, tv shows, and other content through the NOOK Video service. Also, you can use Hulu Plus to see paid content, or watch free video from sites like YouTube, news pages, and other providers.

✔ An optional cable lets you send video and other images from your NOOK HD to a high-definition tv.

✔ A jukebox in a tablet, able to play music you've bought from online sites as well as tunes you already own and have transferred from a desktop or laptop computer.

✔ An art gallery in your hands, capable of storing and displaying photos and videos you've taken with a digital camera or collected from other sources.

✔ A game room where you never have to pick up the pieces, including chess, crossword puzzles, and Sudoku.

✔ Apps (productivity, game, information, and others) you can get — usually for a small fee — from the Barnes and Noble online store.

I did mention that the two models of the NOOK HD aren't quite as fully equipped as a few more-expensive competitors, including a line sold by a company named after a red fruit that can also be made into sauce or juice. Here are a few limitations:

✔ There's no camera.

✔ You'll have to get around without a GPS navigational unit.

✔ Barnes & Noble says it plans to keep its focus on products related to bookselling.

Foolish Assumptions

I assume that you have a NOOK HD or NOOK HD+ tablet — not a NOOK Tablet or a NOOKcolor or a NOOK Simple Touch. This book is about the third generation of NOOKS: the HD and HD+.

I also assume that you have access to the Internet using Wi-Fi in your home or office, and that you can get around on the Internet. And I fervently believe you have (or can use) a personal computer or laptop computer so you can transfer files using the USB cable that came with your NOOK HD or NOOK HD+.

Icons Used in This Book

NOOK HD For Dummies, Portable Edition uses certain art to get your attention.

You could hurt yourself, your machine, or your identity by not following these instructions.

Don't forget.

Let me save you some time, money, or heartache.

Pardon the interruption, but here's a bit of explanation for those of you who want to understand the why as well as the how.

Where to Go from Here

You go just about anywhere you want, of course. You go out of the house and take your book collection and web browser and music and videos with you. You go on planes, trains, and automobiles (as long as you're not the pilot, engineer, or driver). You don't go into the shower or the steam room.

Chapter 1

Viewing in HD and HD+

In This Chapter

▶ Looking at all sides of your NOOK HD or NOOK HD+ tablet

▶ Using microSD cards

▶ Taking care of the battery

*1*n the beginning, there were books. And they were nicely bound between hard covers. Then came paperbacks, which were smaller and portable. They could go with you on trips. But a stack of ten was a heavy load. And engineers built a computer. Then the computers became laptops and were small enough to carry around. Soon, scientists created the e-reader. It was a clever thing — a device about the size of a pamphlet that could hold thousands of books.

Then came tablets. By its evolving definition, a *tablet* has many computer capabilities centered around a touch-sensitive, full-color display that supplies its own lighting. Now, in a technological blink of an eye, we've progressed to HD: high definition, high speed, and highly amazing. And even one step beyond — to HD+, higher and wider.

The NOOK HD and the even more impressive NOOK HD+ represent the third generation of NOOK tablets from Barnes & Noble. They are, hands down, the latest and the greatest in the family. If you've already used one of the older cousins, the NOOK Tablet or the NOOKcolor, you should feel quite at ease with the HD. Quite familiar, that is, in the same way that a 730-horsepower Ferrari F12 Berlinetta is of the same species as a Nissan Versa with a squirrel cage under the hood. They'll both get you to the supermarket, but not quite in the same style or speed.

Telling HD from HD+

The NOOK HD and HD+ both use the same operating system and perform the same functions the same way. But they *aren't* identical twins.

The HD+ is a bit faster, can have more internal storage and, most significantly, has a screen that offers nearly 79 percent more viewing space (and also crams in about 5 percent more dots per square inch).

Table 1-1 shows the most vital of statistics for the two devices.

Table 1-1	NOOK HD Compared to NOOK HD+	
	NOOK HD	*NOOK HD+*
Screen	7 inches diagonal (21 square inches)	9 inches diagonal (37.5 square inches)
Screen resolution	1440 x 900	1920 x 1280
Pixels per inch	243	256
Number of possible colors	16,777,216	16,777,216
Dimensions	7.6 x 5 inches	9.5 x 6.4 inches
Weight	11.1 ounces	18.2 ounces
Thickness	.43 inches	.35 inches
Processor	Dual-core TI OMAP 4470 at 1.3 GHz	Dual-core TI OMAP 4470 at 1.5 GHz
Internal storage	8 or 16 GB	16 or 32 GB
Memory card	As much as 32 GB	As much as 32 GB

Inspecting the Gadget

When you need to type characters or numbers (to move around the web, type in an email address, or the like), a virtual keyboard shows up. When it does, you can tap away at the touchscreen. It isn't tough to use, but I don't want you to get the idea that you can easily use the NOOK HD or HD+ to write the Great American Novel. You can read *The Adventures of Huckleberry Finn* or *The Great Gatsby* with ease and style. See Figure 1-1.

You can read those novels a bit more easily on the larger HD+ screen, but its onscreen keyboard is only slightly better than the tiny equivalent on a smartphone; it's fine for filling in forms, composing emails, and shopping, but it isn't great for touch-typing.

Courtesy Barnes & Noble

Figure 1-1: Reading is easy; typing is tougher.

Find a place in the closet to store the box your NOOK HD or HD+ came in. If you need to send in the device for warranty service, this sturdy protective package is perfect for the purpose. And if you choose to someday regift your tablet to someone else and upgrade to the next wondrous model, it will look so much more impressive if it arrives in its original packaging.

As I say earlier, the HD and HD+ models are nearly identical, but pay attention here to a few tiny differences. All of the following descriptions are based on looking at either model lying on its back, with its top facing away from you and the bottom closest to you: very much like the way you would look at a page from a book.

The front

The front is home to just two or three items of note, two of them quite important and one strictly for whimsy:

- ✔ The HD or HD+ color touchscreen
- ✔ The Home button: ∩
- ✔ The NOOK notch on the NOOK HD+ only: strictly for whimsy

See Figure 1-2 for a guided tour of the larger, faster NOOK HD+. And in Figure 1-3, you can see the similar — but not identical — parts of the NOOK HD.

Figure 1-2: The essential buttons, ports, and slots of the NOOK HD+.

Figure 1-3: A map to the external parts of the NOOK HD.

About the color touchscreen

The color screens on both models are, to use a technical term, drop-dead gorgeous. A few other details are worth noting: The screens use something called *in-plane switching (IPS)*. IPS is an improved version of an *LCD* (liquid crystal display). It offers wider viewing angles and better color reproduction than earlier designs. The NOOK laminates the display to the surface of the touchscreen, which makes for less reflection and glare. The touchscreen uses *capacitive sensing,* meaning that it can tell the precise location of your touch as your finger disrupts the display's electrostatic field. I thought you'd get a charge out of that.

Home button: ∩

The Home button is marked with the NOOK symbol, which looks like this: ∩. If your NOOK HD or HD+ is *sleeping* — with its screen turned off to reduce battery use — the screen is also locked so that accidental touches don't perform actions. Touch the Home button to wake up the device and turn on the screen.

If the screen is already awake, touching the ∩ button takes you back to the Home screen. If you have told the system to require a password to start or reawaken, you will have to enter the four-digit secret code. Once you do that, the NOOK HD or HD+ returns to the screen you were on before it went to dreamland.

If you don't make the NOOK HD or HD+ require a password, you'll need to give the reader a special wake-up swipe. The sleeping device shows a circle on the screen, surrounded by profiles for the users who are allowed to use the device. Touch and hold one of the profile pictures or names, and drag it into the circle to unlock the device and return to the last screen you were viewing.

About the NOOK notch

The NOOK HD+, like its older cousins the NOOK Tablet and the NOOKcolor, has a cute little notch in the lower-left corner. It looks for all the world like a place to hang something — perhaps a mountaineer's carabiner. But please don't. The designers wanted to make their reader immediately recognizable from across the room and this was the artistic element they came up with. Alas, the NOOK HD is notchless, a great loss to us all.

Don't use the NOOK notch to hook the NOOK HD+ to your belt buckle (or to anything else). Although I'm sure some people will think it's cute to attach a rabbit's foot to the notch, let me join with B&N in recommending against it: You just might end up damaging the screen.

The top side

What you see depends on which model you have.

NOOK HD owners see a wondrously simple top. At the right corner is a headphone socket that connects to a common

3.5mm jack for earbuds or to an external sound system. And just next door is a hole behind which lurks the tiny microphone for the tablet. That's it; there's nothing more to see up here.

NOOK HD+ owners: The headphone jack is in the right corner, and about a third of the way over is the hole over the microphone. In between (on the NOOK HD+), you'll see the + and – volume buttons. I know you could figure this out, but here goes anyway:

> + raises the volume.

> – turns down the volume.

The tablet doesn't go to 11.

The bottom

On both the HD and HD+ models, the bottom has a couple important entry points: a specially designed 30-pin port and a microSD memory card slot. And there's a tiny power indicator light. It's orange while you're charging up and it's green when the battery is fully filled.

The 30-pin connector serves three purposes:

✔ Here's where you attach the USB cable that came with your tablet, and that cable, in turn, attaches to the AC adapter, allowing you to recharge the internal battery.

✔ If you buy an optional cable, you can send a high-definition image or video from your NOOK HD or HD+ to a television or other device that accepts an HDMI signal.

✔ You can use the USB cable to connect the NOOK HD or HD+ to a computer to transfer files (a *side load* in technospeak). You can drag and drop any PDF or EPUB files (plus compatible files from word processors, spreadsheets, and presentation programs) from other sources. You can also move files from the tablet to your computer.

If you're comfortable with the basics of a Windows or Macintosh computer, you can attach your NOOK HD or HD+ and use it as a storage device — essentially the same as an external hard drive or a flash memory key. You can also connect to a digital book manager like Adobe Digital Editions or

Calibre to manage files. (I explain book buying and file trans-fer in Chapter 4 of this book.)

The 30-pin connector (such a boring, yet utterly descriptive name) is specific to the NOOK HD and HD+ devices. Be very careful before using any look-alike connector unless it prom-ises full compatibility with your device. You can plug in the connector only one direction — with the little ∩ facing up, aligned with the ∩ on the front of the tablet itself.

The tiny microSD slot opening can accept a little sliver of elec-tronic flash memory (called a *microSD card*) as large as 32GB. This card holds information that's in addition to your tablet's built-in memory. And though 32GB is a whole lot of room, if you fill up one card, you can simply remove it and install a new card.

The left

NOOK HD+ owners won't see a thing on the left side of their tablet.

NOOK HD owners will see the power button on the left side of their device. (HD+ has the power button on the right.)

- ✔ **To turn it on:** Press and hold the silver button for 2 sec-onds (one Mississippi, two Mississippi . . .) and release it to turn it on. If your tablet needs a password, enter that four-digit number.

- ✔ **To turn it off:** Press and hold the little rectangular button for about 2 seconds (one Mississippi, two Mississippi. . .). A message asks if you really, really want to do that; tap the Power Off button to confirm.

You don't have to turn off your NOOK HD or HD+ when you're done using it. It can tell that you haven't tapped its screen for a few minutes. It will turn off its screen and go to sleep. Or, press and immediately release the power button to send it to Sleep mode. The advantage to Sleep is that when you wake the NOOK, it jumps right back to where you were the last time you were paying attention to it.

If you start with a fully charged battery and let it go to sleep, the NOOK HD or HD+ should sleep for a week or perhaps several. (Make sure the Wi-Fi radio is turned off, or the battery will drain even while the tablet is sleeping.)

Why would you want to completely turn off the NOOK tablet?

- ✔ You're on an airplane that's taking off or landing.

- ✔ You're in a hospital or the like.

- ✔ You want to put your tablet on the shelf for a month while you sit down to write your own Great American (or Canadian) Novel.

The right

Okay, so here you have some changes in latitudes and changes in attitudes.

The NOOK HD+ power button is here. For details, read the description of that energetic button in the preceding section, but don't forget that on the HD+, the power button is on the right side of the tablet.

On the NOOK HD, the volume buttons are on this side (not on the top, like they are on the other device). Either way, you know how they work, I'm sure: + means louder and – means quieter, all the way down to mute.

The back

The tablet's back gives the tablet something to hold up the front. And it's where you can find the built-in speakers.

The HD+ has a single opening opposite from the NOOK notch. Two tiny speakers are under the grill. The NOOK HD has no notch, but it does have two tiny openings, with a speaker beneath each grill. You can look at the backs in Figure 1-4 and 1-5.

Speakers

Figure 1-4: The back panel of the NOOK HD+ has a single grill that covers a pair of tiny speakers.

Don't expect the sound quality (or volume) to rival your stereo system. The audio is good enough to hear system notification tones and — with a bit of effort — music or audio. But if you plan to groove to some of your personal tunes, buy earbuds and plug them into the outlet at the top end. If you want to share the sound with someone, you can buy a splitter that allows two devices to plug into the same jack.

If you're going to be listening very closely to music or speech, it may help if you do not lay the tablet flat on its back; to get the best sound, the speaker should not be covered.

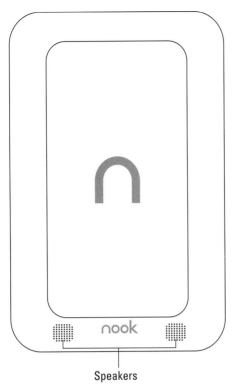

Speakers

Figure 1-5: The NOOK HD back panel has a pair of separated speakers.

Getting More on a microSD Card

SD cards are forms of *flash memory*. That means once you save data, it stays even when the power is turned off.

There are enough kinds of *secure digital (SD)* cards to confuse even the experts. There are SD, mini SD, and microSD sizes, and then there are SD, SDHC (high capacity), and SDXC (extended capacity).

Here's what you need to know:

- ✔ *Do* buy a microSD, microSDHC, or microSDXC card.
- ✔ *Don't* buy an SD or miniSD card.

I recommend buying a card with these specs:

- **microSDHC or microSDXC card.**

- **16GB or 32GB.** You'll get the most bang for your buck with a 32GB card, the maximum size for the NOOK.

- **Class 6 speed.** You don't need to pay for a faster speed (like Class 10), and you don't save enough money to make it worth putting up with a slower Class 2 or Class 4 card.

- **Made by a recognized name brand.** That includes Kingston, Lexar, Sandisk, or Transcend. Cheaper brands exist, but I don't recommend taking unnecessary chances with data.

One example of a microSDHC card is shown in Figure 1-6.

Figure 1-6: This 32GB microSDHC card is from Kingston Technology.

Installing a microSD card

The kind designers of the NOOK HD and HD+ made sure you don't need a post-graduate degree in engineering to install a memory card. You can get to the card slot without removing the back cover; you need no tools other than your fingers.

Just take your time, be careful, and follow these instructions to install a memory card:

1. **Turn off the device.**

   Technically this isn't required, but it is a good practice anytime you're working with electrical devices.

2. **Cover a well-lit, clean, level surface with a soft cloth. Lay the tablet face down on the cloth.**

   Make sure there are no cups of coffee, soda, water, molten iron, or anything else that could spill onto your tablet.

3. **Find the small soft plastic lid to the left of the 30-pin connector on the bottom of your NOOK HD or HD+.**

4. **Using the tip of your finger, gently pull the lid straight out from the body of the tablet.**

   The lid doesn't completely detach; flexible bands keep it on. See Figure 1-7.

5. **Hold the memory card *with the logo facing up toward you;* carefully slide it into the slot.**

   Push gently against the card until it's fully in place. See Figure 1-8. Don't force it into place; if you have the correct memory device (a microSD size card), it should fit easily. If it looks about twice as large as the opening, you've got the wrong card. Micros only need apply.

6. **Gently slide the lid closed and snap it into place.**

Figure 1-7: Open the plastic cover to expose the SD card slot; shown here is the NOOK HD.

To remove a memory card from your tablet, follow the first three steps for installing a card and then carefully slide the card out of its slot. Place the card in the protective case it came in (or in a clean plastic bag) and put it away for future use. Close the small gray lid and snap it into place.

Figure 1-8: Insert a microSDHC card in the slot on the bottom of the device; shown here is the NOOK HD+.

Formatting an SD card

Your new microSD card may come *formatted* (a process that electronically indexes its memory so that the computer inside your tablet knows where to store or retrieve information). In that case, it's ready.

If you insert an unformatted microSD card, the NOOK HD or HD+ will alert you. No biggie: Use the Format command.

To format a microSD memory card when the system asks, follow these steps:

1. Tap the Format Now button.

You're asked if you are sure. Sure you're sure!

2. Tap Format Now.

Babying the Battery

To do all the gee-whiz things, your NOOK tablet needs electrical power. Specifically, it needs a properly charged battery; the good news is that the device's lithium ion battery is rechargeable.

Chances are your new NOOK HD or HD+ will arrive with not much of a charge in its electrical tank. And therefore, the first thing you want to do — after you open the box — is plug it in and put some juice in the battery. If you are really, really determined (impatient?) to try your new tablet as soon as it arrives, go ahead and turn on the power; if there's not enough of a charge, the NOOK will either refuse to start or display a warning message along these lines: *Get thee to a chargery.*

If you turn on your NOOK when its battery is almost gone, you get a warning to begin recharging before you try to use the tablet. If the battery is depleted, the tablet will shut down until it has been sufficiently recharged.

Charging checklist:

✏ The only officially sanctioned source of power for your NOOK HD or HD+ is the AC adapter provided by Barnes & Noble. It comes in the box with the tablet, no extra . . . err . . . charge.

✏ The charger and its cable with a 30-pin connector *aren't* the same as the unit used by older cousins like the NOOK Tablet, the NOOKcolor, or any of the original NOOK e-readers.

✏ You *may* be able to find a replacement AC charger and cable with identical specifications from a third party; check and double-check before using one.

✔ You can buy a car charger from B&N.

✔ You can't charge the NOOK HD or HD+ using the power output of a USB port on a personal computer or laptop.

Getting power from the wall

The NOOK HD or HD+ power adapter is a small cube that you plug into a wall outlet or power strip. To use it, you also need to attach the USB (sometimes called *microsUSB*) cable to the cube at one end and to your tablet at the other. See Figure 1-9.

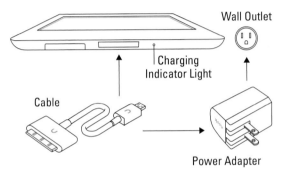

Wall Outlet

Charging Indicator Light

Cable

Power Adapter

Figure 1-9: The power adapter and its detachable USB cable for the NOOK HD or NOOK HD+ look like this.

Follow these steps to charge up:

1. **Plug the smaller end of the USB cable into the right spot on the AC adapter.**

   There's only one opening, and the connector on the cable will only fit in one orientation. The little ∩ symbol faces up, away from the direction of the electrical plugs.

2. **Plug the large 30-pin connector end of the USB cable into your NOOK tablet.**

3. **Plug the power adapter into a compatible electrical wall outlet or power strip.**

   If your NOOK tablet was turned off, it will turn itself on. Depending on how much power is in the battery, it might take 4 hours to fully recharge your device. The indicator light at the bottom of the device turns green when it's fully charged.

The adapter can work with power between 110 to 240 volts; however, the shape of the plug is designed for use in the United States and Canada. You *can* connect your NOOK HD or HD+ power adapter to a *plug adapter,* which lets you plug into a European or other foreign power source that uses a different plug shape. (There are a lot of *plugs* and *adapters* in this paragraph; re-read it carefully if you're going to travel outside the United States or Canada. Otherwise, press on with this chapter.)

Don't turn off the NOOK HD or HD+ while it's charging.

You can also check on the battery by looking at the little battery icon in the right corner of the status bar that appears on the screen of your NOOK tablet. You may need to unlock the device to see the screen; I explain how to do that in the very next section.

If the charging indicator is blinking, something is wrong. One possibility is that the tablet or the adapter is too hot; move it to a cooler place and try again. If it continues to blink, call Barnes & Noble customer service and seek their counsel.

Locking or unlocking the tablet

When you allow (or command) your NOOK HD or HD+ to go to sleep, the screen shuts off to save power. It also locks the touchscreen so you can't accidentally touch or swipe and make it do something.

To wake your NOOK from a doze, do this:

1. **Press the ∩ button at the bottom of the front side of the tablet.**

   If you've set it up so that you have to enter a passcode, tap the number pad to provide the secret code; then tap the Enter key.

2. **Touch and hold on your name or picture; swipe it up into the middle of the circle that appears on the screen with a lock at its center.**

   I explain touchscreen gestures in the next chapter.

   After you unlock the NOOK, you're back to the last screen you visited.

Chapter 2
Going Home on the NOOK

. . . .

In This Chapter

▶ Going to the Home screen, the Recent Drawer, and the Daily Shelf

▶ Getting familiar with the status bar and the system bar

▶ Knowing how to use gestures

▶ Setting user profiles

▶ Configuring your system to your personal preferences

. . . .

The NOOK HD and HD+ each have a tappable, swipable, scrollable touchscreen that allows you to truly enter the virtual world. You can tap a picture of a book cover to read or buy it. You can flick your way through web pages with your pointing finger. You can swipe from left to right (or vice versa) to slide through menus. And you can scroll up or down on a list of options.

If you're upgrading to the NOOK HD or HD+ from an earlier model of NOOK tablet, be ready for the Home screen to look and work a bit differently. The basic concepts and organization are the same, though.

Seeing the Parts of the Whole

Aristotle, who to the best of my knowledge didn't own a NOOK of any sort, is credited with saying, "The whole is greater than the sum of its parts." He said it in ancient Greece and in ancient Greek, but he could well have been considering the beauty of a modern electronic device.

Here's what I mean by that: The whole of the NOOK in either version is made up of hundreds of different screens and features that can be mixed and matched in more ways than I'm able to count. The options screen for the web browser is completely different from the one for the music player, yet they share the same brain and screen and memory. This section goes through the main parts. See Figure 2-1.

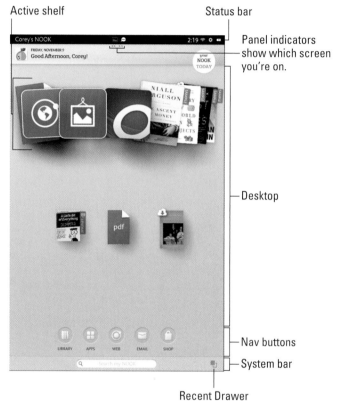

Figure 2-1: The essential elements of the NOOK HD and HD+ Home screen.

Using the Home Screen

The Home screen is like the desktop on a personal computer. The Home screen has five main parts:

✓ **Desktop:** You can change, customize, and update the five panels. Get to the panels by pressing and holding the screen and swiping left or right. The main panel is in the middle of the five; think of it as Door Number Three.

✔ **Active Shelf:** This scrollable electronic metaphor for a bookshelf is at the top of the Home screen. It has anything you've recently bought, obtained, accessed, or otherwise been active with. That includes items you may have borrowed from another NOOK owner using the LendMe feature.

The most recent purchased items are arranged to the right on the shelf; the content you most recently used is presented on the left. Touch and hold an item and swipe left or right to move through them; they'll move as if they were on a carousel.

✔ **Nav buttons:** Just above the bottom of the Home screen, a set of buttons give you quick access — *navigation,* if you prefer — to the major parts of your NOOK HD or HD+.

✔ **Status bar:** A small ribbon at the very top.

✔ **System bar:** Lives at the bottom of the screen.

I explain all five parts, plus more, in the following sections.

You can get back to the Home screen from nearly anywhere with a single press of the ∩ button on the front of the NOOK.

Home screen desktop

As I note earlier, the Home screen is divided into five panels that you can use in most any way you want; only one of the five is active at a time, but the other four are waiting in the wings. You can drag and drop a book, magazine, newspaper, or document to any one of the panels if you want it immediately available for tapping.

Which of the panels are you looking at? Check the easily overlooked *panel indicators* at the top of the screen; they're just below the black status bar in Figure 2-1. You'll see five small circles. The solid white circle shows which panel is active; the other four panels, available but not active, are shown as a gray circles. To move from one panel to another, swipe your finger left or right across the screen.

The nav buttons

Five quick navigation buttons live near the bottom of the Home screen. (If you used the NOOK Tablet or NOOKcolor, you know these buttons as the Quick Nav Bar.) The name has changed but the function hasn't: The nav buttons are the superhighway to some important functions. See Figure 2-2.

To return quickly to the nav buttons, press the ∩ button on the front of the NOOK HD or HD+.

The buttons are titled like this:

- ✔ Library
- ✔ Apps
- ✔ Web
- ✔ Email
- ✔ Shop

Figure 2-2: The quick-access nav buttons take you directly to some of the more important functions of the NOOK HD and HD+.

Library

The Library has your NOOK content, including e-books, magazines, newspapers, catalogs, videos, apps you've bought, and files you've transferred from your personal computer. Like any proper library, you'll find rows of shelves. A brand-new NOOK may not have much piled in those stacks, but it's easy to fill them, and you don't have to do any heavy lifting. See Figure 2-3.

Figure 2-3: A view of the Library shelves, in landscape mode, with the book listings expanded and other shelves closed to save space.

The standard shelves follow:

- ✔ **Books.** If you buy or otherwise obtain a book, it will appear on the Books shelf; catalogs, magazines, and newspapers go on the appropriately named shelves.

- ✔ **Apps.** Those that you buy (or get for free) go here.

- ✔ **Magazines.** If you subscribe to or buy a single issue of a magazine, it will appear here.

- ✔ **Newspapers.** If you get a newspaper, it will appear here.

- ✔ **Catalogs.** If you get a catalog, it will appear here.

- ✔ **Movies & TV.** You can watch both; find them here.

- ✔ **Kids.** They shelf titles are remarkably self-explanatory, although some buyers may want to know that *Kids* refers to children's literature and not to a storage place for young family members.

- ✔ **My Shelves.** Read more about shelves in Chapter 5.

- ✔ **My Files.** The items you've made or transferred are here, including files of text, music, photos, video, or other material. (See Chapter 4 for how to side load items to your NOOK.) This shelf also has screenshots you've captured from the NOOK screen; that semi-secret process is described in the world-famous Part of Tens in this book.

- ✔ **My Scrapbooks.** Here's home for catalog and magazine clippings. As you thumb through many of these colorful periodicals on your NOOK, you can send a particular page to a folder that stays on this shelf. This works only on some periodicals; you can tap to buy something on some, as well. It's frighteningly easy to shop in this way. I discuss Scrapbooks in more detail in Chapter 4.

When you get your NOOK, each shelf is set up to show a small picture *(thumbnail)* or icon representing an item available there: a tiny version of a book cover or a movie poster, for example.

However, you can shrink a shelf to just its name by tapping the arrow on its left:

- ✔ Tap → to expand a shelf title and see the thumbnails and icons.

- ✔ Tap ↓ to close the shelf so you see only its name (and the number of items stored there).

And there's one other arrow: Tap the $\rightarrow$ at the end of a closed shelf to leave the main Library page and go to a full-page display. If you have more items than can fit on a single page, swipe up on the screen to see more.

 Turning off a shelf display in your Library may seem unnecessary, but when you start filling your NOOK with dozens, hundreds, and thousands of files, you'll appreciate the convenience.

Apps

Tap this button to see that your NOOK HD or HD+ is more than a mere e-book reader. If you tap the App button, you can see the NOOK's built-in apps (including Calendar, Contacts, Email, Gallery, Music Player, NOOK Friends, and the web browser), as well as any apps you've bought from the NOOK Shop or otherwise obtained for your device.

I discuss the supplied apps and the B&N NOOK Shop in detail in Chapter 5.

Web

Tap here to open the NOOK web browser and move onto the Internet, through an enabled Wi-Fi connection. Read more in Chapter 6.

Email

Here's a quick route from the Home screen to the NOOK's built-in email manager, which works with most major email services. I get into the details of how it works in Chapter 6.

Shop

Here's your one-tap access to the Barnes & Noble store. Just about every time you visit the site, you'll see a different display; some of the recommendations are based on your previous purchases. I discuss the shopping experience in Chapter 5. If you want to shop at a store not owned by B&N, you'll have to get there by using the web browser.

The shortcuts menu

There's one more menu you can display on the Home screen, as needed. The shortcuts menu — you probably guessed this — is a editable panel of active icons you can tap to jump directly to a particular app or item.

To see the shortcuts menu, press and hold on a blank section of the Home screen; it works best if you choose a place in the lower third of the screen above the nav buttons.

The shortcuts menu has four tabs at the top. Tap one to see the shortcuts; you can scroll left or right to see more.

- ✔ Library
- ✔ Apps
- ✔ Wallpapers
- ✔ Bookmarks

Tap any one of the items to go directly to it. Later in this chapter, I show you how to edit the parts of the shortcuts menu.

 The initial NOOK HD and HD+ user guides promised a fifth tab in the shortcuts menu, called Widgets, in the nav buttons. But the operating system as installed and updated with the hardware didn't have Widgets. Both the user guide and the operating system are certain to go through several updates in the life cycle of the hardware; it's unclear where Widgets will find a home.

Your NOOK Today

When you set up a main profile (or one of the five other profiles you're allowed) on a NOOK HD or HD+, you identify a bit about your interests. And the device also has access to your home address and it can also read the clock. Based on that information, Barnes & Noble offers a daily newsletter that recommends reading material, videos, and apps that are inline with your interests.

To read the newsletter, all you need to do is tap the Your NOOK button in the upper-right corner of the Home screen.

My top headline, shown in Figure 2-4, says, "Good Evening, Corey!" Since it's after dark, there's a little image of the moon — properly adjusted to show a waning crescent that is up there in the night sky over my home. Below that the temperature and weather conditions. Finally, a word from our sponsor: five scrollable panels of books based on my recent activity in the NOOK Library, plus choices based on my interests.

Figure 2-4: My NOOK Today greets me by name, pays attention to the time, temperature, and moon phase, and suggests things I might like to read or watch.

It's interesting and quite unobtrusive: You aren't required to read the advertising newsletter unless you want to see what booksellers and a computer think you might like.

Changing Your Home Screen

You can think of the Home screen (or the *Home page,* as the user guide sometimes calls it) as your desktop or your kitchen counter. If you're at all like me, that brings to mind an image of what seems like totally chaotic disarray. Just like your counter, you can move things around to go from total chaos to organized disorder.

Later in this chapter, I tell you how to make some structural changes to the Home screen. But you start with what lands on the Home screen automatically: Anything you recently obtained or opened will appear on the Active Shelf in the upper third of the screen.

Removing an item from the Active Shelf

If you want to get rid of something from your Active Shelf, do this to remove them:

1. **Press and hold on the thumbnail or icon for reading material or an app on the shelf.**

   A submenu opens.

2. **Tap Do Not Show On Home.**

   The selected item disappears. Now you can add items to the Home screen.

Adding an item from shortcuts to the Home screen

You can put almost anything in your NOOK's memory on the Home screen for quick access, including books, magazines, newspapers, videos, and apps.

You can also add bookmarked web pages as well as *widgets,* which are utilities that show things like clocks and calendars. The difference between a widget and an app is pretty minor; think of a widget as an app specifically designed to appear on the Home screen.

To add an item to the Home screen, do this:

1. **Press of the ∩ button to go to the Home screen.**

2. **Press and hold on a blank part of the Home screen.**

   The shortcuts menu opens.

3. **Tap Library, Apps, Wallpapers, or Bookmarks.**

4. **Press and drag on the item to move it into place.**

   See Figure 2-5 to see a book in the process of being moved. You're just moving a copy of the icon.

5. **Tap the Done button at the bottom of the shortcuts menu.**

Figure 2-5: I'm moving an item from the Shortcut menu to the Home screen's desktop.

Removing an item from the Home screen

If it started on the Home screen, you can't take it from there. However, if you added something to the Home screen, you can take it away:

1. **Press and hold on an item.**

   A pop-up menu appears.

2. **Tap Do Not Show On Home.**

Checking Your Status Bar

The status bar runs across the top of screen and shows up on many pages of the NOOK HD or HD+. See Figure 2-6 for an example of the status bar. On some pages, the status bar stays out of the way to keep from distracting you.

To make the status bar appear on a page where it's hidden, tap at the top of the displayed page. For example, when you're reading an e-book, tap above the top lines of text. I suspect the availability and actions of the status bar will change over time as Barnes & Noble refines the operating system that runs the latest models of the NOOK.

The status bar on the NOOK HD and HD+ looks and acts different from earlier versions for older NOOK devices. When describing the status bar, I divide up the information by left, center, and right side.

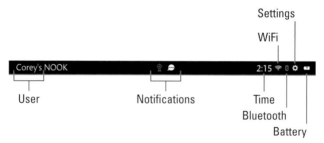

Figure 2-6: The status bar lives at the top of the screen, filled with tiny bits that take you to useful information.

Left

No, your other left.

The left part of the status bar has the user's name. For example, the main profile on my NOOK HD+ shows "Corey's NOOK." Assuming you don't need help remembering your name, this tidbit simply tells you which user profile you're using. Some NOOK owners may have only one profile, but others may let family or friends set up their own profile. I discuss profiles in Chapter 4.

Center

This is the notifications area. If your NOOK wants to (or needs to) tell you something important, a small icon will appear here. Tap the icon to see details.

The notifications can include the following:

- Downloads are ready; a downward-pointing arrow tells you that updates are coming to your device. No need to worry. This is all perfectly normal.

- You have an email (if you've registered the account to your NOOK).

- A NOOK Friend has asked to borrow something from your Library.

- Something technical, such as SD card formatting, is afoot.

- An system software update is available.

- Barnes & Noble sent you a message, including recommendations for books or other content you might buy.

Right

On the right side of the status bar, you'll find the following:

- The current time. Make sure you know what time zone you're in. The official time on your NOOK HD or HD+ is used for updates, downloads, and synchronized bookmarks.

- A Wi-Fi indicator. If it's bright white, you're connected to a router. The higher the stack of little curves, the stronger the signal. No curves equals no connection. Two or three curves are a good connection. If the indicator is gray, your device is either out of range of a Wi-Fi router or you've turned off the NOOK's radio system. I discuss Wi-Fi in more detail in Chapter 6.

- A Bluetooth indicator. This wireless technology is for short-distance communication between the NOOK and devices like earbuds and keyboards. The B symbol is blue if Bluetooth is turned on and connected; the B is pale if the system is enabled but not connected.

- The gear symbol. This is your direct entry to the Quick Settings panel. From there, you can make some basic adjustments or tap All Settings to see everything within your configuration grasp.

✔ An icon that shows the status of your NOOK's battery. If the battery icon is completely white, it's fully charged. If the NOOK is attached to the AC adapter, a tiny green lightning bolt in the battery tells you the battery's being recharged.

Seeing What's Stocked in the System Bar

The system bar is at the very bottom of many screens. The system bar will appear on the Home screen, the Library, the Shop, and the Settings panels. The system bar has a search tool, plus other special-purpose tools that vary from screen to screen. See Figure 2-7 for an example.

Figure 2-7: The system bar, at the bottom of many screens, lets you search (and do other things) depending where you are on your NOOK.

The following sections have a few examples of the system bar.

Home screen

When you're on the Home screen, the system bar has these goodies:

✔ **A Search tool** that scours the contents of your NOOK's memory for a particular book, a name or word, or an app. If you're currently connected to an active Wi-Fi router, the tool will also hunt in the Barnes & Noble store and go out on the web. You can tap any result to go to that item. See Figure 2-8 for an example.

✔ One or the other of these reading tools:

• The **Recent Drawer,** represented by two overlapping squares.

• Your **most recent reading material,** represented by an open book.

Figure 2-8: I modestly searched for my own name and found listings in my Library, the NOOK Shop, and the web; you can control where you search from Settings.

Library

In the Library, the system bar has this:

- ✔ A **Library icon** (it has four stacked lines) that you can tap to open the Library menu. From there you can quickly create or reorder shelves, manage content for profiles, and control reading material archiving.

- ✔ A **Search tool** that will look through your NOOK's memory, the web, and the Barnes & Noble shop.

- ✔ One or the other of these reading tools:
  - The **Recent Drawer,** represented by two overlapping squares.
  - Your **most recent reading material,** represented by an open book.

Shop

When you're in the shop, the system bar has a few extra bells and whistles. See Figure 2-9.

- A **WishList icon** (a heart) that you can tap to see you're the items you covet.

- A **Recents icon** (a shopping bag and a clock) that shows items you've recently looked at.

- A **Search tool** that looks high and low through the Shop for whatever name, title, or subject you type in the box.

Recents
WishList

Figure 2-9: The search in the Shop brings up a WishList and recently viewed items, shown as icons at lower left.

✔ One or the other of these reading tools:

- The **Recent Drawer,** represented by two overlapping squares.

- Your **most recent reading material,** represented by an open book.

Returning to Recent Reads

Your NOOK HD or HD+ comes with quick access to items and places you've visited recently. You get to choose between two types of indexes, which I explain in the following sections.

Recent Drawer

You can get to the Recent Drawer in the system bar; tap the icon of two overlapping rectangles. The Recent Drawer is a horizontally scrolling panel that shows the last 50 items you have opened. By items, I mean e-books, movies, pictures, videos, and all manner of maps.

To go back to any one of these items, tap its thumbnail; the Recent Drawer will close and the chosen item will open.

Recent Read

If you prefer, you can use the awkwardly named Recent Read. This index doesn't let you choose items: If you tap that icon, you go directly to the most recently read page of a book or other material.

Here's how to make the change:

1. **Pres the ∩ button to go to the Home screen.**

2. **Tap the gear icon in the status bar.**

   The bar is at the top of the page. The Quick Settings menu opens after you tap the icon.

3. **On the menu, tap Home Settings.**

4. **Tap the check box next to Show My Recent Drawer. The check mark should be gone.**

The option is in the section called Quick Corner Action.

5. **Pres the ∩ button go back to the Home screen.**

6. **In the system box at the bottom of the screen, you'll see the icon for Recent Read.**

To revert from Recent Read to Recent Drawer, follow the first three steps, and then tap the check box beside Show My Recent Drawer.

Keeping Your Gestures Polite

I'm not talking about using your hands or fingers in a particular way to express your opinion of a great work of literature or the latest piece of pointless piffle by a pompous politician. The gestures are pretty easy to master, and you've got no choice: They've taken away your keyboard, mouse, fountain pen, stylus, and chisel.

I cover the basic gestures here. Not every page offers the same features, but you'll quickly learn how to tap-dance your way anywhere you want to go.

Tap

A *tap* is a quick strike by the tip of your finger. Think of poking at a key on a computer keyboard. Let me show you how in Figure 2-10.

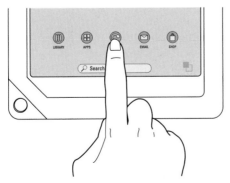

Figure 2-10: Tapping or double-tapping a button or part of a screen usually takes you places.

Double-tap

Bet you figured this one out, right? A *double-tap* is two quick pokes by the tip of your finger.

- ✔ If you're at the Home screen, Library, Recent Shelf, and some other pages, double-tapping a book cover shows details about the item. You get the same result double-tapping a book cover in the B&N online bookstore.

- ✔ On the web or in the picture gallery, double-tapping an image zooms you in. The same happens when you're reading a PDF file, including some books that are stored in that format.

- ✔ Double-tapping an enlarged image or page from a PDF or web page will return the image or page to its original size.

- ✔ Double-tapping other icons scattered here and there will either open a description, start an app, or move to the next level in a multilayer shelf.

Press and hold

Touch a finger to the screen and hold it there for two seconds. Oh, and then lift your finger off the screen; your finger doesn't have to become a permanent part of your NOOK HD or HD+. On some other tablets and smartphones, the press-and-hold gesture is called a *long press*.

Depending on the screen, a press and hold usually opens a pop-up menu that offers choices based on what you're doing or where you are.

- ✔ Press and hold a book cover and then release to show a menu with options such as Open the Book, Recommend It, or Lend It.

- ✔ Press and hold on an item on the Daily Shelf to get the opportunity to remove the book from display.

- ✔ Press and hold, then lift, from a word in a book to open the Text Selection toolbar. You can then look up a word in the NOOK dictionary or go online to Wikipedia or

Google. The same toolbar lets you add a note to the beginning or end of a passage in a document, or to bookmark that page.

✔ Press and hold on the cover of a book or periodical in the Library to send that publication to the *NOOK Cloud.* (That's your personal archive. The material isn't deleted, but you can't see it in your current reading material.) Or, you can delete a file using the same menu. I discuss the NOOK Cloud in Chapter 5.

✔ When you're typing, press and hold a letter on the virtual keyboard to see accents, diacritical marks, and special characters.

✔ To open a file stored on a microSD memory card, go to the Library, tap the My Files icon, and press and hold a filename.

✔ Press and hold on the Home screen wallpaper to choose a different background image: one of your own pictures, a picture that came with your NOOK, or a *live* (animated) scene.

✔ In the music player, press and hold to add a track to a playlist.

Swipe

I'm not advising you to steal a book. *Swiping* in this case means sliding your finger across the screen. See Figure 2-11. Think of it as using the left- or right-arrow keys on a computer keyboard. You can swipe to the left or to the right; you get a different effect depending on what type of file is open or where you are on the NOOK.

Here are some examples of a swipe in use:

✔ In the Recent Shelf, Daily Shelf, or your Library, swipe to move through a collection of items (such as a row of book covers).

✔ When reading, swiping to the left will flip the page forward. Swiping from left to right takes you back a page.

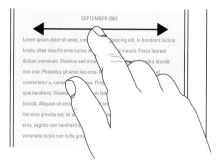

Figure 2-11: Swipe to move side to side.

Scroll

A *scroll* is a vertical swipe; you move your finger up or down on the screen to go through a list. Think of it as using the up- or down-arrow keys on a computer keyboard. See Figure 2-12.

For example:

- Scroll up or down through a list of menu options.
- Move down or go back up to a set of small images of books, book pages, bookmarks, photos, or songs.
- Go through a magazine article or a web page in Article View, zipping through the text without illustrations or photos.

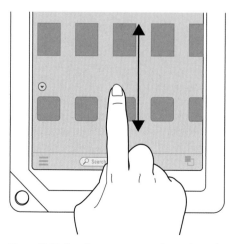

Figure 2-12: Scroll to move up or down through a list.

Drag

When you *drag* on a touchscreen, you are — in an electronically metaphoric way — touching an object and pulling it to another location. Touch an object and keep your finger on it as you drag it where you want it to go; when the object (an icon, for instance) is where you want it, lift your finger from the screen to leave the object in its new location.

Drag to these ends:

✔ Drag to move parts of a website that's outside of the borders of the NOOK screen.

✔ Drag an icon from one part of the Home screen to another, or from the Active Shelf to the Home screen.

✔ Drag a slider left or right (or up or down) to adjust things like volume.

✔ Zip through the pages of a book by dragging the location slider right or left.

✔ Select a phrase by dragging a vertical bar (at either end of a word) until a pair of bars are around it.

✔ Drag crop marks to frame the part of an image you want to keep.

✔ Drag the icon for your profile into the circle in the middle of the start screen to unlock the tablet and see the Home screen.

Lift

You *lift* your finger from the screen when you're done making certain gestures such as dragging or pressing and holding. I tell you this just as a precautionary measure so that you don't feel you have to walk around for the rest of the week with your finger pressed tightly to the touchscreen.

Pinch

Ouch! A *pinch* is where you touch the two fingers on the touchscreen and bring two of them toward each other (or away from each other — aka a *pinch out*). Most people use their thumb and pointer fingers. Pinch your fingers toward each other to shrink an image — a book cover or a photo, for example. Spread your fingers apart to zoom in on or enlarge an image on the screen. See Figure 2-13.

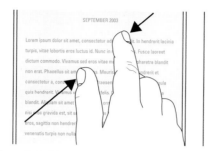

Figure 2-13: Pinch to zoom in or out on text or an image.

Press

The NOOK HD or HD+ have just four physical buttons: switches that you actually press. You don't tap, swipe, pinch, or anything else — just press.

- The first is the power button.
  - **NOOK HD+** is at the top of the right side.
  - **NOOK HD** is at the top of the left side.
- A pair of + and - volume buttons.
  - **NOOK HD+** is on the top edge.
  - **NOOK HD** is on the upper section of the right edge.
- The ∩ button sits at the bottom of the screen as you hold it in portrait mode. Hooray: same place, both devices.

Using the Virtual Keyboard

One of the truly amazing things about using a tablet is the lack of a keyboard. Of course, there *is* a keyboard; it's virtual and context-sensitive. What does that mean? *Virtual* means the keyboard responds to taps similar to how a computer keyboard does but is actually only a picture on the screen. And the keyboard is *context sensitive;* the keyboard only appears when you need it to fill in a form or an email message or other situations where letters, numbers, and symbols are required.

The standard keyboard is the familiar QWERTY layout used in the United States, Canada, and elsewhere. As the NOOK HD or HD+ is released in other parts of the world, you can expect other virtual keyboards to be offered: In France, the AZERTY design is more common, for example.

You can switch keyboards by doing this:

- ✒ Switch from lowercase to uppercase by tapping the ↑.
- ✒ Switch from characters to numbers by tapping the ?123 key.

On many keyboards, you can see an accented character or a special symbol by pressing and holding a key for a second or so. In Figure 2-14, I present a menagerie of keyboards.

Figure 2-14: A set of context-sensitive virtual keyboards from the NOOK HD+.

Chapter 3

Setting Things Up

In This Chapter

▶ Setting up profiles

▶ Making settings for the system software

▶ Handling storage

*O*ne of the true benefits of working with a computer —
and make no mistake about it, the NOOK HD and HD+
are computers beneath the skin — is being able to customize
and adjust the way they look and work. In this chapter, you
explore user profiles and settings for the system software.

Styling and Profiling

Profiles are one of the biggest changes to the operating
system for the NOOK HD and NOOK HD+. Each NOOK can support as many as six profiles, which lets different people use
the tablet in different ways or with different permissions.

Your NOOK HD or HD+ has three kinds of profiles:

- ✓ Primary
- ✓ Adult
- ✓ Child

The primary profile

You must have at least one profile; the primary profile is created automatically when you first register your NOOK. The primary user has these privileges and responsibilities:

- ✔ This user can see everything on the device; there are no hidden sections.

- ✔ This user can make or edit all of the other profiles on the device.

- ✔ This user gets all the bills. Anything bought from the NOOK Shop is billed to the credit card or other payment method associated with the device. You have to authorize your credit card when you register your NOOK.

The primary profile is created during the initial registration of your NOOK HD or HD+. You'll create or link an existing Barnes & Noble account with the device and give some feedback about your interests (so it can customize parts of the online Shop just for you).

Your NOOK must be connected to a Wi-Fi network for you to be able to create, edit, or delete a profile.

An adult profile

We're all grown-ups here, right? An authorized adult with a profile can

- ✔ Buy and see any type of content.

- ✔ Set restrictions that keep other users, including children, from seeing any material associated with the profile.

There's one exception: The holder of the primary profile sees all and knows all. And the bill still gets sent to the person responsible the primary profile.

To create a new adult profile for your device, do this:

1. **In the upper-left corner of the Home screen, tap the name of the profile currently in use.**

The primary profile is usually automatically set up to use the first name of the responsible owner; on my device, the primary profile is called Corey's NOOK.

A window shows the primary profile, as well as any other profiles already created on your device. On the same panel you will see two buttons: Add Adult Profile and Add Child Profile.

2. **Tap Add Adult Profile.**

   The NOOK opens a form.

3. **Fill out the form. See Figure 3-1.**

4. **Tap His or Her.**

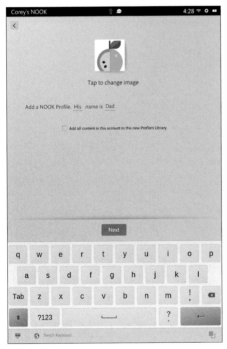

Figure 3-1: You can have as many as six profiles on your NOOK; a primary plus five others authorized to adults or children.

The first release of the user guide says that identifying the sex of a profile holder is optional; the initial version of the operating system makes you choose for adults but not children.

5. **Type a name for the person who will be using the profile.**

   Because this person isn't responsible for paying the bills, you can choose any name you want.

6. **Decide whether to tap a check mark next to Add All Content In This Account to This New Profile's Library.**

   Leaving the box blank mean this profile's content will have only items that the new user adds and not everything already on the device.

7. **Tap one or more areas of interest for the profile owner.**

   Depending on what choices you make here, Barnes & Noble will offer samples of reading material in hopes you will buy it.

8. **Tap Next to finish.**

A child profile

A child who's given a profile can only see or buy content allowed by an adult profile or primary profile owner. The child can't create or edit other profiles or override any parental controls. And, of course, the bill for purchases still goes to the person who created the primary profile.

To create a new child profile, do this:

1. **In the upper left of the Home screen, tap the name of the current profile.**

   A window shows the primary profile, as well as any other profiles already created on your device. Two buttons are on the same panel: Add Adult Profile and Add Child Profile.

2. **Tap Add Child Profile.**

   The NOOK opens a form.

3. **Fill out the form.**

4. **Tap the line that reads Boy/Girl.**

5. **Choose A Girl, A Boy, or (to maintain some privacy) A Child.**

6. **Type a name for the person who'll use the profile.**

7. **Tap an age and enter a month and year of birth.**

   The age can range from a newborn infant to 18 years. Federal COPPA (Children's Online Privacy Protection Act) regulations apply.

8. **Tap the open box to place a check mark and accept the terms and conditions related to a profile for a child.**

   The NOOK shows a menu of parental controls for this profile. See Figure 3-2.

9. **Tap check boxes to set limits:**

   - Browse Shop
   - Password-Protect Purchases in Shop (This means the person trying to buy something has to type a password.)
   - Display Only Kids Content in Shop
   - Access My Files in Library
   - Browse the Web
   - Reads for Kids
   - Apps for Kids
   - Videos for Kids
   - Games for Kids

10. **Optional: Adjust limits for purchase and video viewing by selecting age-related ratings.**

    Your NOOK automatically selects ratings based on the child's age. Movie ratings for children include G, PG, and PG-13. TV ratings for children include TV-G, TV-Y, TV-Y7, TV-PG, and PV-14.

11. **Tap Continue.**

    You'll see possible interests for the child.

12. **Select interests.**

    The Shop offers sample content based on the choices.

13. **Tap Done.**

Do you want to require the child to enter a passcode to access the NOOK? If the idea is to keep a child from accessing the content and privileges in an adult profile, the process — at least in the initial release — falls short. Instead, the lock prevents *any* user from getting onto the NOOK HD or HD+ without the proper code. After the passcode is entered, anyone can switch to a different profile.

In practice, if you are going to allow a child to have his or her own profile, you're going to have to be there to supervise and assist. That's not the worst thing, as you help a youngster discover the joys of reading. But until Barnes & Noble fine-tunes the operating system, one lock fits all.

Figure 3-2: The primary profile holder can set parental controls for children ages infant to 18.

Changing or deleting profiles

Only the primary profile owner can edit other adult profiles and child profiles. And an adult profile can only edit his or her own profile. A child cannot edit other profiles.

The only profile that cannot be deleted is the primary.

To edit or delete a profile, do this:

1. **In the upper left of the Home screen, tap the icon for the current profile.**

   A window will open with the names of all profiles that have been created on your NOOK.

2. **Tap the Edit Profile button.**

   Icons of editable profiles will change color to indicate they can be changed.

3. **Tap the profile you want to edit.**

4. **Tap an option:**

   - **Change Interests**

   - **Change Image** (Icon or thumbnail that represents the user.)

   - **Manage Content** (Allow or deny access to books, magazines, apps, videos, and other items.)

   - **Remove This Profile**

   - **Change Parental Controls** (Child profile only)

Setting Up Your NOOK the Way You Like

Unlike a printed book or a tv set, you can change your NOOK HD or HD+ in almost unlimited ways. You can change the way screens appear and respond, organize your files, and make your tablet match the location and way you use it.

The basic control panel is the Quick Settings panel. In the status bar, tap the gear icon. See Figure 3-3. You can make basic changes there; tap All Settings to see all the settings.

Figure 3-3: Basic settings you may want to use regularly are on the Quick Settings panel; to burrow deeper, tap All Settings.

If you tap the gear icon from the Home screen, you'll have one additional option on the Quick Settings panel: Home Settings.

The Quick Settings panel

The Quick Settings options are the ones you're likely to change. To change the way the device itself responds, you'll need to open All Settings.

The following sections explain the Quick Settings panel.

Home Settings

This option only appears if you open Quick Settings from the Home screen.

Brightness

Press and hold the little button on the slider and move it left to darken or right to brighten the screen. Some users like to have a dimmer screen in low-light situations (like reading in bed).

Wi-Fi

Tap the toggle switch to turn on or off the Wi-Fi radio. When you turn it on, you may see available networks to which you can connect; choose one with a strong signal. I discuss Wi-Fi in more detail in Chapter 6.

Airplane Mode

Tapping this switch turns off your device's Wi-Fi and Bluetooth radios (also discussed in Chapter 6), to quickly meet the requests of airplane pilots. The advantage of using this switch is that it leaves Wi-Fi settings unchanged.

Lock Rotation

Tap the switch to lock the screen in its current orientation, either portrait (tall) or landscape (wide). Your NOOK won't change orientation if you hold the tablet differently.

All Settings

Tap here to go into the internal settings for nearly every feature of your NOOK HD or HD+. Not to worry; I'll be your guide.

All settings

The main NOOK HD or HD+ settings are made up of six parts: Wireless & Bluetooth, General, Applications, Account Settings, Storage Management, and Device Information.

Wireless & Bluetooth

This page has three switches to control your NOOK's radio circuitry. See Figure 3-4.

Figure 3-4: This is the main control panel for the Wi-Fi and Bluetooth radio.

- **Airplane Mode:** Turns off your device's Wi-Fi and Bluetooth radios.

- **Wi-Fi:** Turns it on or off. When it's On, the NOOK looks for networks and shows what it finds. You'll see three important bits of information:

  - The name of any found network.

  - A closed lock icon to show any network that isn't available to you without a login and password.

  - The signal strength for the available networks. The more curved lines in the stack, the faster and more reliable the communication will be.

  Select a network and, if you haven't already, type a login name and password (if they're requested). After then, you should see a message that your device is connected to the Internet. I discuss wireless communication in more detail in Chapter 6.

- **Bluetooth:** This communication is for short distances. If you turn on Bluetooth, you have to allow it to be "seen" by devices in the area, and then arrange for them to work together. You can find more details in Chapter 6.

General

Here is where you can change many operations. See Figure 3-5.

Figure 3-5: General Settings has many of the hardware operations of the NOOK HD or HD+.

The options include the following:

- ✔ **Battery Life.** Tap the toggle switch to turn on or off PowerSave mode. When on, the screen is a bit dimmed, and some of the power to the Wi-Fi and Bluetooth radio systems is lower. Don't use this setting if your NOOK is connected to the AC adapter, or if your NOOK is too slow or unresponsive when using the battery. You can manually reduce the screen brightness to save power.

- ✔ **Lock Rotation.** Tap the toggle to lock the screen in its current landscape or portrait orientation. That way, you can lounge on the couch without the screen flip-flopping.

- ✔ **Brightness.** This has nothing to do with your tablet's IQ, but rather with the backlighting. Drag the slider from dim to bright or back. A bright light might help in a dark room, but you may strain your eyes; a dimmer backlight may help you read outdoors. In any case, lower brightness uses less battery power. Choose the lighting level that works best for you and adjust it as needed when conditions change.

✔ **Screen Timeout.** Tap this option and then choose how long the NOOK will wait before it goes to sleep; the clock only starts to run when the device doesn't get any taps or other gestures from you. Available options run from two minutes to one hour.

You get a few seconds' notice before the tablet goes to sleep: The screen dims slightly. When the screen shuts off, turn it back on again by pressing the ∩ button and swiping your profile name into the circle.

✔ **Language.** Tap here to see instructions in a particular language. Initially, the NOOK HD and HD+ offered only languages English (United Kingdom) and English (United States). You can expect other languages as the device is more widely available.

✔ **Personal Dictionary.** Add words that you'd like the tablet to recognize; it's more like a spelling checker for email and other messaging.

✔ **Keyboard.** The NOOK HD or HD+ will eventually offer a number of keyboards with special characters and symbols as used around the world.

✔ **Text-to-Speech Output.** The NOOK can read aloud certain types of text; this feature is used in some children's books and may become a feature for the visually impaired. You can adjust the speech rate and listen to an example of the device reading at normal speed or two levels slower or faster.

✔ **Pointer Speed.** Well, your NOOK has neither a mouse nor a trackpad, but you can adjust the speed that the hardware reacts to your finger on the screen, which is the tablet's substitute for a mouse.

✔ **Sounds.** Any settings you make here affect the volume range, but a physical volume button on the NOOK itself lets you turn up or down a sound as it plays.

 • **Set Volume** for music and videos.

 • **Set Volume** for notifications.

 • **Alarms** for, you know, alarms.

Tap the switch to turn on or off the sound that you hear when the system institutes a screen lock.

✔ **Security Settings.** You have two options here.

- **Security.** Tap Security and then tap the toggle switch to turn on or off a screen lock. If you turn it on, you have to type a number passcode; choose one that isn't so obvious as your phone number (but not so obscure that you might forget it). Your passcode can have as many as 16 digits.

Want a good reason to add a device lock passcode? Your Barnes & Noble account stores your credit card number. That means someone else could buy something at B&N without your permission, although whatever he bought would wind up on the device associated with the account.

- **Certificate Management.** I suggest you change this setting only if a technician or system manager insists on it. Don't play around here without assistance.

✔ **Date & Time.** You can adjust the time zone, turn on or off 24-hour format for time, and select a date format. See you at 17:30 for cocktails in the office lounge.

The system clock is used for the alarm and calendar apps. It's also part of the synchronization process. Some systems may reject your NOOK's attempt to communicate if they see you're using an incorrect date or time. Make sure you correctly set the date and time; you don't want to accidentally get rid of books.

✔ **Notifications.** Tap the switch to turn on or off the display of notifications on the status bar — things like downloads, emails, and system alerts.

There's nothing wrong with a bit of experimentation; if you change something and it winds up in behavior you don't like, come back here and undo it. But for that reason, I suggest you make notes on changes you institute, and only put one or perhaps two into effect at a time. See if the device is working the way you want before making additional adjustments.

Application settings

The application settings help you customize some of your NOOK's personality, the part that runs on your NOOK as well as some of the supplied apps.

Home settings

There's no place like it. And the Home settings page lets you decorate and organize to make it as comfortable and productive as possible. See Figure 3-6.

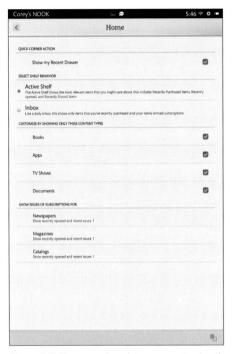

Figure 3-6: Home settings lets you customize the types of reading and viewing material on the Home screen. You can see more items in the NOOK Library.

The Home settings page has four settings. Here's what you can do in each:

- ✔ **Quick Corner Action.** This one is a bit awkwardly designed.

  - **Show My Recent Drawer.** If you tap to put a check mark in this box, you'll see a pair of stacked rectangles in the lower-right corner of the Home screen (plus some other pages on the NOOK). Tap the boxes to see a scrollable bar of items you've looked at; the latest is at the left, the oldest at the far right. You can tap any one of them to revisit it. See Figure 3-7.

- **Recent Read.** If you remove the check mark from the box, the icon in the lower right of many pages will be an open book with a tiny clock. This replaces Recent Drawer. Tap the icon to go to the very place you left off reading in the very most recently visited book, magazine, catalog, or other item on your NOOK.

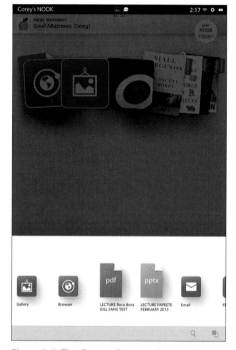

Figure 3-7: The Recent Drawer shows all manner of items or apps consulted in the not-too-distant past.

✔ **Select Shelf Behavior.** Oh, behave your shelf. Choose between one of two options for a secondary shelf on the Home screen:

- **Active Shelf.** Select this and you'll see the NOOK's judgment of the most relevant items for you, including Recently Purchased, Recently Opened, and Recently Shared items.

- **Inbox.** Select this for a customized daily inbox, showing only items you recently bought as well as recent issues of magazine and newspaper subscriptions.

✔ **Customize Content Types.** Which types of items do you want to see on the Home screen? Tap to place a check mark alongside any or all of these content types: Books, Apps, TV Shows, or Documents.

✔ **Show Issues of Subscriptions.** Tap Newspapers, Magazines, or Catalogs and decide about how many, if any, periodicals you want displayed on the Home screen. Your choices are none, 1, 2, 3, or All.

Email settings

You can add new email accounts and manage some existing ones. Account names and addresses are in a column on the left. I discuss using email in more detail in Chapter 6.

When you set up an email account on the NOOK, you can name each account (Corey's Mail, for example) or use the email address (something like *mymail@privateaddress.tvu*).

In the main section of the Email panel, you can choose the following:

✔ **Auto-Advance.** Tap here to open a menu and tell the system what to do after you delete a message: advance to a newer message, to an older message, or to the main list of messages. There's no right or wrong answer here; choose the one that makes the most sense to you.

✔ **Message Text Size.** Tap one of five relative type sizes: tiny, small, normal, large, or huge.

✔ **Reply All.** If you tap a check mark into the box, Reply All is the default for message replies. That means if you get a message that was sent to many people, your reply doesn't go only to the original sender but also to everyone else on the list. In my opinion, this *isn't* a good practice; you can reply to all recipients on an email-by-email basis. It's safer (and more considerate) to ordinarily send any reply only to the original sender.

✔ **Ask to Show Pictures.** If you turn on this option, your system won't automatically download pictures sent to you as part of an email. Instead, you'll see a message asking if you want the pictures to be shown. Turning off the automatic download will make your email run faster and save space in memory.

✔ **Add Account.** Tap the button at the bottom of the page to add a new email account. You're asked to enter an email address and password and then choose automatic or manual setup. I discuss this in more detail in Chapter 6.

Calendar settings

The NOOK HD and HD+ have a full-featured Calendar app that you can coordinate with your system clock, alarm, and email. However, you have to use the Microsoft Exchange service, a product that's sold mostly to businesses and organizations.

✔ If you have a Microsoft Exchange account, follow the onscreen instructions to link your NOOK to the Exchange Calendar.

✔ If you don't have a Microsoft Exchange account, you can subscribe. The service is based on your PC, and then you can connect to it from a portable device such as a NOOK HD or HD+ or a smartphone.

The instructions for setting up a Microsoft Exchange account on the NOOK are very straightforward. Among your choices are which day to use as the start of the week, a home time zone, and control over notifications. See Figure 3-8.

What if you don't have and don't want a Microsoft Exchange calendar? You have two options:

✔ Buy a calendar app from the NOOK Shop. These calendars usually work quite well alone, not linked to your email or contacts and aren't something you can share with other users.

✔ Use the web browser and connect to an online calendar such as Google Calendar or Yahoo! Calendar. Each lets you integrate to its own email services (Gmail and Yahoo mail). And as a bonus, many of these online calendars can be shared with others and can also be made to sync with calendars that run on smartphones.

In mid-2012, Microsoft invested in a new joint venture with Barnes & Noble. B&N is expected to offer NOOK reading applications for tablets running Windows 8, and B&N just might offer tablets that use a version of Microsoft operating systems (instead of the current Android-based software that was developed by Google).

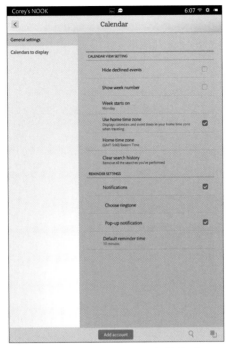

Figure 3-8: The built-in calendar is limited to users who have a Microsoft Exchange account (at least in the initial release).

Contacts settings

The NOOK HD or HD+ can work with contacts you bring in *(import)* from major online sites such as Facebook and Google Gmail. You have to send your contact list from the online site and then store that information on the NOOK.

Or, you can add names and other information by tapping the Add Contact button within the Contacts app. Tap the Contacts app to see your current contacts; tap the icon in the lower corner (a tiny person with a + mark) to add new information. See Figure 3-9.

The Contacts page comes ready to accept a name, organization, phone, email, and address for each contact. You can also tap the human head beside the Name field, and choose an image from the Gallery on your NOOK to put a face or a picture with the contact. Finally, you can tap Add Another Field to insert more information, such as instant messaging address, notes, nicknames, or websites.

Figure 3-9: You can type contacts from the NOOK or send them from elsewhere.

The first release of the NOOK HD or HD+ didn't have the Contacts registry fully implemented. Check with NOOK support for updates.

Browser settings

You can make some basic changes here; with the built-in web browser itself running, you can go to a full menu that offers more settings. Here are the custom settings:

- ✔ **Set Homepage.** Tap here to decide which page to see when the NOOK browser is turned on. You can set the homepage from the browser itself.

The settings you choose in the Browser menu are only for the built-in app that comes with your NOOK. If you add a third-party browser such as Dolphin, that browser will have its own setup.

✔ **Form Auto-Fill.** Tap in the check box to have the NOOK fill in some web forms using information you've entered before; this generally applies to your name and address, not to passwords and sensitive data. If you're concerned about security, you might want to leave this box unchecked.

✔ **Auto-Fill Text.** If the previous option is selected, tap here to open a screen with fields you can fill in; the NOOK will use this information to automatically enter text in online forms. See Figure 3-10.

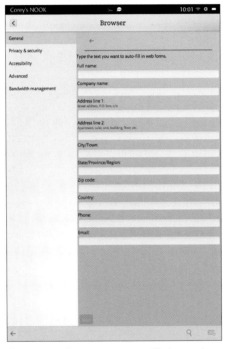

Figure 3-10: If you turn on auto-fill, the entries you make in this panel are matched to requests from websites.

Magazine/Catalog/Comics reader

The NOOK HD and HD+ really shine when it comes to colorful magazines, catalogs, and comics. You can turn on or off a few super powers:

✔ **Enable HotSpots.** Tap to put a check mark if you want to let the tablet respond to interactive hotspots on the page; that means things like jumping to a web page, animating a character, or otherwise astounding and amazing you.

✔ **ZoomView Letterboxing.** Tap to put a check mark if you want to automatically fit odd-shaped pages onto the screen of the NOOK HD or HD+. Without this feature, some pages may look too small or overlap the screen.

✔ **Page Turn.** Choose between two nifty page-turning animations: curl or slide. Try them both and see which impresses you and your friends the most.

Shop

You have control over several purchasing powers and a few security or privacy features.

✔ **Password Protect Purchases for Adult Profiles.** Tap a check mark here to make sure all adult profile users must enter a second password before they can buy something from the NOOK Shop. This requirement should help prevent a stranger from running up a tab. To enable or disable passwords for child profiles, go to the Profiles panel on the Home screen.

✔ **Manage Credit Card.** You can change the credit card that you use to pay for purchases at the NOOK Shop. There can be only one default card. See Figure 3-11.

✔ **Gift Cards.** If you get a gift card, you can add the card (or certificate number and its PIN) through this section. When the card is added to your account, you'll see the total balance here.

The gift card balance is automatically applied to your next purchase; if it can't cover your order completely, your default credit card covers the remaining cost. You can have a maximum of three gift cards, eGift cards, or online gift certificates in your account at any one time. If you have extra cards, keep them safe and add them after you've used other balances.

If you have questions about or problems when you're trying to use a gift card, call Barnes & Noble customer service at 1-800-843-2665. Those last four digits spell BOOK, by the way.

Figure 3-11: There can be only one credit card associated with the B&N
account, but the primary profile holder can change it from this
panel. And no, that is not my real credit card number.

✔ **Clear Recent Shop Searches.** If you don't want the next
person who uses your NOOK to know what you've been
looking at recently, tap here to erase the record.

✔ **Clear Recently Viewed List.** Similarly, to remove the
record of items you've recently looked at, tap this option.

Social accounts and NOOK Friends

To some, the web is their oyster. Social networking on
Facebook and exchanging life's minute details with Twitter fit
seamlessly into the world of NOOK Friends; see Figure 3-12. If
that describes you, here are the missing links:

✔ **Manage Your Accounts.** Tap here to link your Facebook
or Twitter accounts, which allows quick message
exchange. It also lets you make or accept LendMe offers.
Type your login and password details for each service.
Missing from the NOOK HD or HD+ operating system, at

least in its initial release, is synchronization with Google Gmail accounts.

✔ **Add Facebook Friends as NOOK Friends.** Tap in the check box to turn on this feature. If you've set up a Facebook page, and you've been friended those you know best (and some who know you least), add their information so they can share books, recommendations, and comments using the NOOK Friends network.

Figure 3-12: To use the social features, including LendMe, you have to link your system to a major network, like Facebook or Twitter.

Reader

Reader is the app that lets the NOOK Tablet read e-books. Most of Reader's functions are set (or you can adjust them on the pages of books and magazines). But on this page, you have a few other options:

✔ **Enable Sliding Animations for Page Turns.** This tiny bit of micromanaging is one that some readers really enjoy: A check mark in this box (it comes this way) makes an e-book's pages slide smoothly across the screen as you turn. Or, you can choose the next option.

✔ **Enable Curl Animation for Page Turns.** Put a check mark here to have the system present a nifty animation that makes pages curl in one corner as they turn. You've got to choose slide or curl; you can't have check marks in both boxes.

✔ **Enable 2-Page PDF Display Mode in Landscape.** This is simpler than it sounds. Place a check mark here if you want any PDF file to show as a two-page spread (like an open magazine). It works if you hold the NOOK in landscape mode (wider).

✔ **Dictionary Options.** The standard dictionary for the NOOK HD or HD+ is the *Merriam-Webster's Collegiate Dictionary,* Eleventh Edition. Someday there may be alternate dictionaries offered for English or other languages. Until then, leave this setting untouched.

Search

Now where in the world did I put that magazine, and how can I find the song I bought because of the profile of the artist I read there? You can tell the Search tool where to hunt. You can also clear recent searches so they don't reappear as suggestions when you start a new hunt.

Tap to place a check mark beside any of the places shown here; remove the check mark to avoid looking in that location. See Figure 3-13. Some apps that you get from the NOOK Shop will show up here in addition to the built-in features of the tablet.

Figure 3-13: On this settings panel you can instruct the NOOK where to look when you ask it to conduct a search for a name, item, or title.

Here are some of the places searches can go:

✔ **Web.** Look on the Internet as well as in your browser history and bookmarks.

✔ **Apps.** Include the names of applications you've installed.

✔ **Contacts.** Look for the names and information of contacts you've added.

✔ **Hulu Plus.** Search movies, tv shows, and videos offered at this NOOK-approved web service.

✔ **Library.** Hunt for book titles, subjects, authors, and other information in the Library.

✔ **Music.** Look for information in the filenames and other details of songs on your NOOK.

✔ **Office Suite.** Search for information in files and other data recorded by this app, which allows you to read certain word processing, spreadsheet, presentation, and other files created on a computer.

✔ **Shop.** Look for results in the NOOK Shop, including books, videos, and apps.

NOOK Video

A control panel for the NOOK Video service is scheduled to be here. For a bit more detail about that service, see Chapter 6.

Account settings

This small section of the Settings panel will likely grow over time as Barnes & Noble adds more connections external services. As first delivered, it offers just two.

UltraViolet

Once Barnes & Noble and UltraViolet get all of the kinks worked out, this will be where you can link your UltraViolet account to your NOOK HD or HD+. Until then, all you see is a placeholder.

UltraViolet lets you buy video content — a DVD or a digital download — and watch it on a wide range of devices: televisions, tablets, smartphones, and devices we don't even know that someday we absolutely must own. See Chapter 6 for more details about UltraViolet.

Adobe Digital Editions

Here you can add or activate an ID for use with Adobe Digital Editions, an app that lets you add copy-protected e-books from libraries and from shops other than the one owned and operated by Barnes & Noble. I discuss Adobe Digital Editions in more detail in Chapter 5.

Storage Management

You can see, at a glance, the available storage space in your NOOK HD or HD+. You have storage space in two places:

- ✔ The built-in *(internal)* storage that comes with your device. It's just there.

- ✔ The contents of a microSD card if you have installed one in your tablet. See how to do that in Chapter 2.

The NOOK HD comes in models with 8 or 16GB of internal storage. Of that amount, about 5 or 13GB is available by users; the remainder is reserved for the basic workings. On the NOOK HD+, models come with 16 or 32GB of internal storage. Available space is 13 or 28GB after the operating system has taken its place.

On the Storage Management settings page, you can see a report on total available space. Tap the → to see how much of the space is taken by books, apps, computer files, and other material. See Figure 3-14.

Most users won't need to venture into the USB Connectivity section, but if a technician tells you to, you can choose between a pair of protocols for transferring media files between a personal computer and your NOOK. Here are the options:

- ✔ **Media device (MTP).** This standard setting generally allows easy transfer of media files from a Windows or Mac machine. Most users won't need to change from this standard setting.

- ✔ **Camera (PTP).** Certain devices may require use of Picture Transfer Protocol (PTP) to move photos using proprietary camera software.

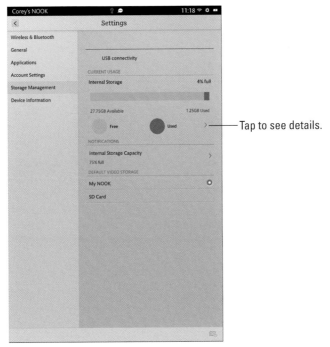

Tap to see details.

Figure 3-14: The front page of the storage management settings shows the space you have left; tap the → beside Internal Storage to see details.

Device Information

This screen mostly shows information; a technician may direct you here to check on the version of operating system software or for details of account, model number, serial number, and Wi-Fi radio address. One other option here — an important one — allows you to erase and deregister your device. See Figure 3-15.

Here are the standard offerings of this screen:

- ✔ **Owner.** The name of the registered owner of the NOOK.

- ✔ **Account.** The email address that's used as the account name; you can use an account on several devices and on NOOK apps that run on personal computers and smartphones.

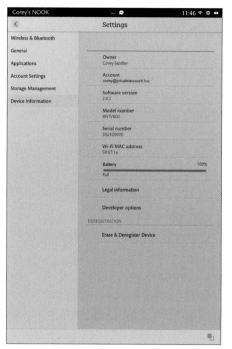

Figure 3-15: The Device Information page has information about the owner and the NOOK's serial number; steer clear of the Erase & Deregister command.

🖊 **Software Version.** The current edition of NOOK operating system software in use on the device.

🖊 **Model Number.** Each NOOK has its own model number; a technician may ask to know yours to confirm whether you have an HD or HD+ model and how much internal memory is installed.

🖊 **Serial Number.** The unique number assigned to your device. It helps tracking it at customer service.

🖊 **Wi-Fi MAC Address.** Have you ever wondered how a wireless system knows how to find you in a crowded room? It keeps track of your NOOK's assigned MAC address.

🖊 **Battery.** A precise measurement of the percentage of charge left in the internal battery. If you tap the Battery line, a graphic tells you which parts of the system are drawing the most power; the two largest users are usually the screen and the Wi-Fi radio system. See Figure 3-16.

If you're really, really bored and are completely ~~anything else to read, you might want to peruse~~ gal notices and credits listed here. Or perhaps you omething to help you fall asleep.

~~oper~~ Options. Although you can take a look at the ~~otions~~ offered here anytime you so desire, I would rec- ~~o~~mmend you make no changes unless you are directed to do so by a technician. These settings may be of use in troubleshooting an unusual problem; don't create one by making changes on your own.

✔ **Erase & Deregister Device.** Stop. Wait. *Don't* tap this option unless you have a *real* good reason to do so. If you tap here, any personal files that you've moved to the NOOK HD or HD+ will be deleted from the device. Also, all e-books are deleted; the details that your device uses to identify itself to the Barnes & Noble website are deleted, too. (Any titles you bought from B&N are linked to your account, and if you re-register your NOOK to that account, the previously deleted books go back onto your NOOK.)

You may want to use Erase & Deregister in two situations:

- Your device gets corrupted or unresponsive and customer support suggests you use it.

- You sell or give your NOOK HD or HD+ to some-one else and allow them to create their own B&N account and pay for their own stuff.

Figure 3-16: If you go down one level in Device Management, you can see which hardware or software is using more of your precious battery.

Chapter 4

Mastering the Reading Tools

In This Chapter

▶ Getting around in your reading material

▶ Using the reading tools

▶ Scrapbooking the electronic way

▶ Making your own book

▶ Side loading new files

*W*hen Moses descended from Mount Sinai with the two most famous tablets, the inscription on them was chiseled in stone. So were the replacement set after Moses smashed version 1. In the nearly four millennia since then (give or take a few centuries; consult your local biblical scholar if you must) there have been many other forms of communication: drawings on papyrus, quill pens on paper, and printing presses among them. And now we all find it perfectly reasonable to obtain our information by decoding dots of light on an electronic screen. Another form of tablet, of course.

But in the end, it really doesn't matter what medium you use to get your message across. The technology is merely the means of transport for ideas. The NOOK HD and HD+ are merely another way to read the printed word and absorb its content into our souls.

Enough of the philosophical discourse; it's time to read on your NOOK. In this chapter you explore the wide array of reading tools that are built into the NOOK HD and HD+. With them you can turn the pages, zoom to a specific chapter, search for words or terms, make notes, place bookmarks, and much more.

This chapter looks at the NOOK HD and HD+ tablets as e-readers: find, open, read, bookmark, scrapbook, and reshelve documents. Then I tell you how to stock the shelves, and how to *side load* (move) books, documents, and other files from your personal computer to your tablet.

Turning Pages in Books, Magazines, and Newspapers

I'm going way out on a limb here and guess that you'd actually like to do some reading: books, magazines, newspapers, and catalogs. Good news! That's just about as easy as tapping your finger. But wait, there's more: You can make notes about what you're reading. You can highlight favorite passages. You can place multiple bookmarks within the book. And you can share your literary criticism or recommendations with friends using websites like Facebook.

Here are the very basics:

- ✔ Tap any icon that looks like a document (from the Home screen, the Library, or file folders) to open a document.

- ✔ Tap or swipe to turn pages. (I explain the details in a moment.) Figure 4-1 shows a page from a fine book.

- ✔ The books you read most recently are in the Recent Drawer (see Chapter 2), but even if they're off that list and back to your Library, you can return to the exact page you last read.

A Little Bit of Everything For Dummies, 20th Anniversary Edition

portant button is the shutter release, or shutter, button. Press it firmly and steadily. Don't jab at it, or else you'll shake the camera.

Figure 11-3: Push a button and get a treat.

- **Knobs:** You'll more than likely have to remove a hand from the camera to turn a knob, as shown in Figure 11-4. It shows the Mode dial on my Sony Alpha 300.

Figure 11-4: Knob turning requires a few fingers.

- **Wheels:** Spin with your thumb or other free finger.

133 of 283

Figure 4-1: Here's a sample page of text and art as seen on a NOOK HD+ screen. The book is the compendium *A Little Bit of Everything For Dummies.*

Opening an e-book

In Chapter 5 I explain more about the book-buying process. But for now, I'm going to make the not-foolish assumption that you've already bought or downloaded a few titles.

Naturally enough, you begin reading by opening a book. To do that, try either of these methods:

✔ Press the ∩ button and tap any cover on the Home screen. Not all books are displayed here, though — just those you recently added or used, or those you put in the more permanent space that occupies the middle third of the desktop.

✔ Go to the Library to open the folder; there you can find books you have purchased or obtained from the Barnes & Noble website, from other online sources, or those that have been brought over to the device from a personal computer or laptop.

Turning the pages

Don't lick your finger and try to turn the page; that's unsanitary and will streak the glass. Instead, here's how to move within an e-book:

✔ **To turn to the next page, tap anywhere along the right edge of the page.**

✔ **To turn to the next page, swipe to the left.** Think of this as flicking a page from the right side of an opened book to flip it over. To go forward one page, place your finger on the right side of the page and keep it in contact as you slide it to the left.

✔ **To turn back to the previous page, tap anywhere along the left edge of the page.** Swipe to the right to go to previous pages. To swipe right, place your finger on the left side of the page and slide it to the right (flicking a page, in an electronic way).

✔ **Use one of the advanced tools.** What are they? Read on.

Understanding page numbering

You may see a page number on the screen. That's helpful, but it may or may not correspond to the printed version of the book (in either the hardcover or the paperback version). In any case, because the type may be larger than what's in the printed edition, and the screen is smaller than the paper, a single page on your NOOK may spread across several screens or digital pages. In some designs, you may "turn" page 47 three times before moving to page 48.

Here's the trick to comparing notes between two e-readers, or between an electronic and a printed copy: Ask for the wording of a particular passage and then find that same passage on your NOOK by using the Search (also called Find) function.

Moving rapidly from place to place

With a printed book, you can flip through the pages, jumping in seconds from page 38 to 383. With an electronic book, it's easy — but different. The following two sections explain quick ways to move from place to place.

Slip, sliding along

One of the basic tools is the page slider; tap anywhere on the page to display it on the NOOK HD or HD+. The slider will appear at the bottom. See Figure 4-2.

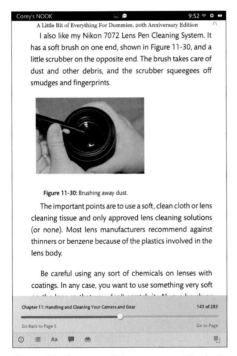

Figure 4-2: The page slider appears at the bottom of a book if you tap anywhere on the page.

The slider shows up as a horizontal line with a white dot somewhere along its path. The location of the dot shows where you are in the book. To the left of the dot, the line is marked in blue to show you the earlier pages of the book; to the right of the dot, the line is gray.

To move forward or backward quickly, touch and drag the slider right or left. If you're reading a book that someone has loaned you, a button at the right end of the slider lets you buy your own copy.

Go to Page

Follow these steps to quickly jump to a particular page in an e-book:

1. **Tap anywhere on the text.**

   The page slider appears.

2. **Tap the Go to Page button.**

   The button is in the lower-right corner of the slider. A numeric keypad appears.

3. **Type a specific page number.**

   Keep in mind that page numbering is relative. See Figure 4-3. If you've changed the font or its size, the page numbers will change.

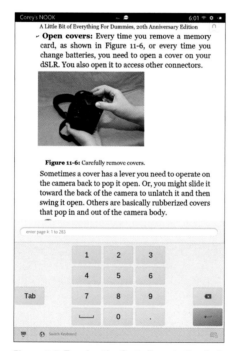

Figure 4-3: Tapping the Go to Page button in the slider panel lets you enter a specific page number.

Mastering advanced e-book navigation

Maybe you don't know what page you want. Instead, you'd like to consult the table of contents. Or perhaps you'd like to search the book. Or you've decided that the typeface is too small or the page background is the wrong color. These are all fine thoughts, and with an electronic device like this one, your wishes are the NOOK's command.

1. **Tap anywhere on the page of text.**

   The main reading tools open, including the slider.

2. **Tap an icon in the status bar.**

You can see some of the icons in Figure 4-4.

✔ **Details.** The letter *i* in a circle is a nearly universal symbol for information. If you ever go too far in Hvar, look for that *i;* it's the local Croatian tourist bureau. Here on the NOOK HD or HD+, though, it means, "Tell me more about this book I'm reading." You'll see a full page description of the book if you tap this icon; some also show reviews and special content.

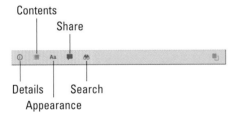

Figure 4-4: When the reading tools are displayed at the bottom of a page of text, they include a set of specialized icons for navigation, search, and appearance.

✔ **Contents.** This icon is a stack of four horizontal dotted bars (actually, they look like the letter *i* once again, only laid on their side). The Content Panel is home to a bunch of navigational tools; when you tap the icon, you'll see three tabs at the top of the panel. I deal with each of them here.

- **Table of Contents.** This is what you'll see first, a listing of the structure of the book, sometimes with subsections. You can scroll up or down through the listing, and best of all: The entries are active. The current chapter is highlighted by a gray bar. In most books you can jump immediately to a section by tapping the title or subsection name. See Figure 4-5.

Figure 4-5: You can see a book's table of contents and easily jump to another section by tapping a chapter title.

- **Highlights and Notes.** These are the electronic equivalent of scribbles or color underlines. You don't have to engage in literary defacement. Instead, the NOOK will keep track of your notes for you. And even better, you can jump to any of your notes or highlights by tapping the item.

- **Bookmarks.** An electronic bookmark works just like a piece of cardboard between pages: It lets you quickly open to a particular page. You can set as many bookmarks as you like in each book.

✔ **Appearance.** The Aa icon this is the entryway to changing how your text looks. Choose from eight type sizes, six typefaces, three line spacing and three margin options, and six background color choices. I explain more about changing the appearance of text a bit later in this chapter.

✔ **Share.** This icon looks like a cartoon character's word bubble. Reading can be a solitary activity, but there's also a longstanding tradition of book clubs and sharing amongst friends. Barnes & Noble was one of the pioneers in the use of social media as a part of the e-book experience, and that has extended to the NOOK HD and HD+ tablets. See Figure 4-6. When you tap the Share icon, you see these choices:

- **Recommend.** Praise a book to friends and acquaintances by sending email, posting a recommendation on your Facebook wall (or that of a friend who granted you that permission), or tweeting through your Twitter account.

- **Post Reading Status.** You can tell others how far you've gotten in the current book by posting a message on Facebook or Twitter. Why? I'm really not sure, but someone must be interested.

- **Rate and Review.** Send your comments and a 1–5 rating for display on www.BN.com, or post your review on Facebook or Twitter.

- **Like on Facebook.** Proclaim to the world (or at least those who read your Facebook news feed) that you really, really like this book.

Before you can use email or social network services, you have to link your NOOK to your Facebook or Twitter accounts or add email accounts to the Contacts application.

✔ **Search.** Tap the binoculars to bring up a virtual keyboard with space to enter a word or phrase. Then tap the magnifying glass on the keyboard (the designer seems to have mixed metaphors here) to find any use of the word or words in the current book or magazine.

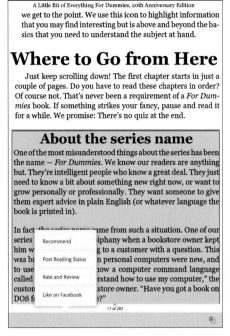

Figure 4-6: Go ahead, share. You can recommend a book and otherwise inform a waiting world of your reading interests and accomplishments.

Finding More Reading Tools

There's a whole other pathway to the bells and whistles: That path lies in the Reading Tools menu. From there, you can move quickly through a book, search for something specific, share your knowledge, or change the way the page looks. I call these the *secondary reading tools,* but actually they're part of the same toolkit.

To see the secondary reading tools, press and hold on a word or anywhere on the page. It might take a few tries to get the hang of it: Tapping will bring you the full set of tools, including the slider bar, while a more determined press and hold brings up the secondary reading tools. See Figure 4-7.

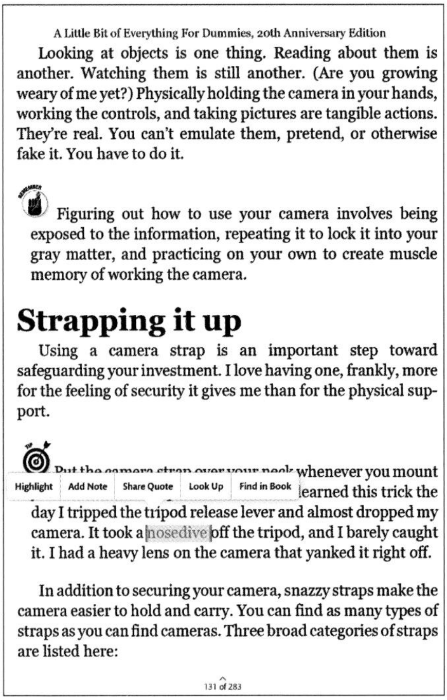

A Little Bit of Everything For Dummies, 20th Anniversary Edition

Looking at objects is one thing. Reading about them is another. Watching them is still another. (Are you growing weary of me yet?) Physically holding the camera in your hands, working the controls, and taking pictures are tangible actions. They're real. You can't emulate them, pretend, or otherwise fake it. You have to do it.

Figuring out how to use your camera involves being exposed to the information, repeating it to lock it into your gray matter, and practicing on your own to create muscle memory of working the camera.

Strapping it up

Using a camera strap is an important step toward safeguarding your investment. I love having one, frankly, more for the feeling of security it gives me than for the physical support.

Put the camera strap over your neck whenever you mount

| Highlight | Add Note | Share Quote | Look Up | Find in Book |

learned this trick the day I tripped the tripod release lever and almost dropped my camera. It took a nosedive off the tripod, and I barely caught it. I had a heavy lens on the camera that yanked it right off.

In addition to securing your camera, snazzy straps make the camera easier to hold and carry. You can find as many types of straps as you can find cameras. Three broad categories of straps are listed here:

Figure 4-7: Press and hold to reveal reading tools that are a direct route to adding notes and highlights and conducting searches.

The tool highlights a word if that's what you've touched; it highlights a nearby word if you've pressed on a blank spot. Above the highlight you will see the buttons described in the following sections:

- Highlight
- Add Note
- Share Quote
- Look Up
- Find in Book

Highlight

To select a word, press and hold on a word; then lift your finger. The word will be highlighted in a blue block, and you'll see a darker blue vertical bar on either side of it (unless you've chosen a different color theme for the page).

To expand the highlight, tap and then drag one of the vertical bars; this tool is called the Text Selection tool. When you lift your finger or fingers (you can use your thumb and pointing finger to cover more area), the Text Selection toolbar appears.

You can't directly print a passage from your NOOK HD or HD+ (at least not in the initial release), but here's what you can do: Select a passage and send it to yourself by email. Then use a computer and printer to make a hard copy.

Be sure you understand the proper use of citations if you're using part of a copyrighted book in an academic paper or a publication of your own.

Add Note

You can insert a comment (up to 512 characters) about the highlighted word or phrase; the date and time are included. A small icon that looks like a sticky note will appear beside the right margin of the page.

- ✔ You can search for what's in your note.
- ✔ You can view and change notes any time.
- ✔ You can also make them invisible. Why? Perhaps you want to share a selection or loan a book to someone but keep your comments private. See Figure 4-8.

To perform other actions on a note you've already made, use the primary reading tools. Here's how:

1. **Tap anywhere on the page.**

   The slider bar and system bar appear at the bottom of the page.

2. **Tap the Contents icon.**

   The icon looks like a stack of four dotted bars.

3. **Tap the Highlights and Notes tab if it isn't already selected.**

4. Tap one of the notes.

You're taken to the page where it's attached.

5. Tap the highlighted word on the page.

A menu appears. See Figure 4-9.

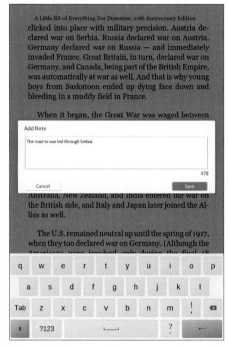

Figure 4-8: You can add notes to an electronic document; you can search notes later.

Here are the actions you can perform from that submenu:

- ✔ **View Note.** Tap to read the comments you placed there.

- ✔ **Edit Note.** Tap here to see the comments onscreen. Use the virtual keyboard to make changes. When you're done, tap Save.

- ✔ **Remove Note.** Tap the command and the note is deleted; there's no second chance, so be sure this is what you want to do.

✐ **Remove Highlight.** Tap to take away the color highlighting. The color shading disappears immediately, but you can always press on the word and reinstall a bit of a hue.

✐ **Change Color.** Tap one of three colors (aqua, lime green, or sunset yellow) to make a change.

A Little Bit of Everything For Dummies, 20th Anniversary Edition
clicked into place with military precision. Austria declared war on Serbia. Russia declared war on Austria. Germany declared war on Russia — and immediately invaded France. Great Britain, in turn, declared war on Germany, and Canada, being part of the British Empire, was automatically at war as well. And that is why young boys from Saskatoon ended up dying face down and bleeding in a muddy field in France.

When it began, the Great War was waged between two opposing alliances:

✐ **The Allies:** Great Britain, France, and Russia
✐ **Central Powers:** Germa, [View Note] Hungary, and the Ottoman Empire (Turk [Edit Note]
The conflict soon grew and [Remove Note] nvolved every ocean and every inhabited co arth. Canada, Australia, New Zealand, and [Remove Highlight] d the war on the British side, and Italy and joined the Allies as well. [Change Color]

The U.S. remained neutral pring of 1917, when they too declared war on Although the Americans were involved o the final 18 months, they did provide a m nflux of fresh troops and supplies, which helped tip the balance in the Allies' favour.)

"Back by Christmas!"

250 of 283

Figure 4-9: You can view, edit, remove, or change the look of notes or highlights.

Share Quote

You can share a word or pick up a short passage and send it by email (or Twitter or in a Facebook post). The NOOK is ready, willing, and able to assist.

When you tap Share Quote, here are your choices:

- ✔ **With Contacts.** This sends the quote using the Email app to contacts you have previously added.

- ✔ **To My Facebook Wall.** Your erudite observations (or those of an accomplished author) will be posted onto the metaphorical wall of your Facebook page, if you have one and have linked it to the NOOK system.

- ✔ **To a Friend's Facebook Wall.** This is an electronic form of graffiti. If your friend has granted you this permission — and if you've linked their Facebook page information to the NOOK system — you can post a quote on a friend's wall.

- ✔ **To Twitter.** Apparently the world is holding its breath, awaiting your latest observation of 140 characters or fewer; if you have linked your Twitter account, you can send a quote as a Tweet to all of your followers.

Look Up

At the risk of repeating myself with an example I've used in other books, what exactly is a battologist? I mean, really, *what exactly is a battologist?* If you come across a weird word, look it up in the built-in copy of the *Merriam-Webster's Collegiate Dictionary,* Eleventh Edition. But if that dictionary can't help you answer the question, "What exactly is a battologist?", then go out on the web to consult other resources. See Figure 4-10. What exactly is a battologist? Someone who unnecessarily repeats something.

From the dictionary page, you can also ask the NOOK HD or HD+ to hit the web:

- ✔ Tap the g icon to use Google, which should deliver page upon page of entries.

- ✔ Tap the W icon to go to Wikipedia; believe it or not, although there are (as I write this) more than 23 million Wikipedia entries, 4 million of them in English.

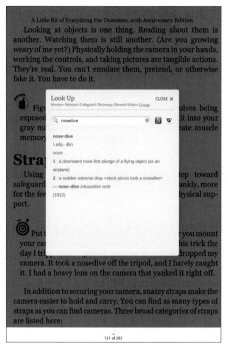

Figure 4-10: The built-in dictionary defines many words, but you can jump onto the web and search Google or consult Wikipedia.

Find in Book

Think of Find in Book as an automated, nearly instant, highly specific indexing tool. If the word, name, or phrase you want to hunt for is already highlighted, tap Find in Book; the NOOK will come back very quickly with a list of anywhere in the book it can find the search item.

From the results page, you can tap any of the findings to jump directly to its location; the word, name, or phrase will even be highlighted for you.

While your NOOK is in the search mode (or mood), you can also enter a new search term in the bar that appears at the bottom, or move forward or backward through the list by using VCR-like controls. Tap X to exit from the search and return to reading.

The Advanced Course in Bookmarks

The following sections explain how to work with bookmarks.

Bookmark the page you're reading

Tap in the upper-right corner of the page. A small blue ribbon appears in the corner of the page. To make the bookmark go away, tap the blue ribbon in the upper-right corner of the page.

See all the bookmarks in a book

Follow these steps to see everything you've bookmarked:

1. **Tap the center of the page to open the reading tools.**

2. **Tap the Contents icon.**

3. **Tap the Bookmarks tab (in the Content pane).**

   You can see all the bookmarks in the book. See Figure 4-11. Tap anywhere on the page outside the list of bookmarks to close the list.

   To jump to a page you have bookmarked, tap a bookmark in the list.

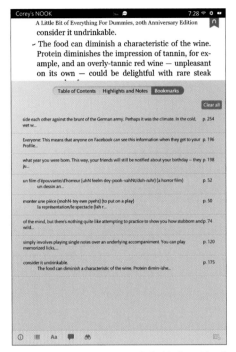

Figure 4-11: You can see a clickable list of bookmarks as well as high-lighted words and notes you put in the text.

Clear all bookmarks in a book

Follow along to get rid of all the bookmarks in a single book:

1. **Tap the Contents icon.**
2. **Tap the Bookmarks tab.**
3. **Tap the Clear All button.**
4. **Tap OK.**

Clipping Pages for a Scrapbook

One of the new NOOK HD and HD+ features is the scrapbook. It can hold entire pages that you want at hand for future reference. In its initial version, the scrapbook is for magazine and catalog pages only, and not all periodicals support the new feature.

Saving a page in a scrapbook

To save a page from a magazine or catalog, do this:

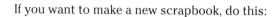

✔ Swipe down the center of the screen using two fingers.

✔ Tap in the center of the page to open the Reading Tools panel. If the periodical lets you scrapbook, you'll see a pair of scissors; tap the scissors.

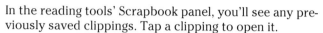

In the reading tools' Scrapbook panel, you'll see any previously saved clippings. Tap a clipping to open it.

If you want to make a new scrapbook, do this:

1. **Tap the New Scrapbook icon. See Figure 4-12.**

   The keyboard will appear.

2. **Type a name for the scrapbook.**

3. **Tap OK when you're finished.**

Figure 4-12: The new scrapbook feature lets you clip whole pages from a catalog or magazine, which can help with your shopping or research.

Viewing a scrapbook

To look at what's in a scrapbook, do this:

1. **Press the ⋂ button to go to the Home screen.**

2. **Tap the Library button.**

3. **In the Library, scroll to the section called My Scrapbooks.**

4. **Tap the scrapbook you want to open.**

Adding a note to a scrapbook page

To attach an electronic note to a page of the scrapbook, do this:

1. **Press and hold on the center of the page.**

   A menu appears.

2. **Tap Note.**

   A dialog box and keyboard open.

3. **Type your note.**

   For example, on the scrapbook page in Figure 4-12, I might type "Does this make me look fat?"

4. **Tap Save.**

Seeing notes attached to scrapbook pages

To see the notes you have attached to a scrapbook page, do this:

1. **On any page in the scrapbook, tap in the center.**

   The reading tools appear.

2. **Tap the Contents icon.**

   A menu appears.

3. **Tap the Notes tab if it isn't already selected.**

Moving through your scrapbook

Once a scrapbook is open, you can perform the following actions:

- **Turn pages** by swiping left or right.

- **Move through pages** by tapping in the center of the page to display reading tools. To see thumbnails of all pages in the scrapbook, tap the grid icon. To see a table of contents or notes for the magazine or catalog, tap the Contents icon.

- **Zoom in** on a page with a double-tap; to **zoom out,** double-tap again.

- **Bookmark a page** by tapping the + sign in the upper-right corner of the page.

Removing a page from a scrapbook

To remove a page from a scrapbook, follow the steps in "Viewing a scrapbook" and then do this:

1. **Go to the page you want to remove.**

2. **Press and hold in the center of the page.**

   A menu appears.

3. **Tap the Remove button.**

Designing Your Own Book

Gutenberg could never have imagined this. This menu, for reasons known only to the designers at B&N, has a different look and feel than most of the other options screens in the tablet. Never mind, though; it's pretty easy to use. See Figure 4-13, which shows the boxes.

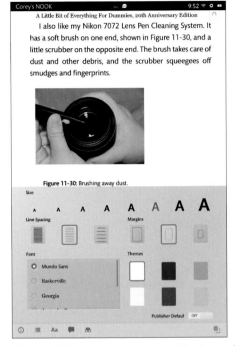

Figure 4-13: Design your own page of book text: Choose type size and style, line spacing, margins, and background color.

Size

In most EPUB books, and in many PDFs, you can choose from eight type sizes. (I explain EPUB and PDF files types, or formats, later in this chapter.)

You just see eight A characters. Start out at the fifth or sixth largest for a good balance between readability and number of words that fit on the page. Feel free to experiment, though; touching any of the As will instantly change the size of the type that shows above the menu.

Line Spacing

You can adjust the amount of space between lines of text: single spacing, 1.5-line spacing, and double spacing.

Margins

Experiment here between narrow, medium, and wide margins for the text. The more white space there is around the text, the fewer words will fit on each line.

Font

The NOOK HD or HD+ comes with six different type styles. (Some book publishers may limit the options, though.) Feel free to experiment with the fonts to find the one that you find easiest to read. Most are similar to those on your personal computer.

Three of the typefaces are *serif* style, like the face used in most newspapers and magazines; many of the characters have extra little straight or curved marks that many readers find to be easier to read. The others are *sans serifs* fonts, which means "without serifs."

Themes

With an advanced e-reader and a color LCD, you can choose the "paper" and the lighting:

- **Day.** This is your basic black text against white background.

- **Night.** You guessed this: white type against a black or gray background. This may be useful for reading at night or in other dark environments where you don't want to light up the room with your book.

- **Gray.** Black text on a light gray background. It isn't a bad occasional choice to rest your weary eyes.

- **Butter.** A slight variation on day, using dark brown text against a pale yellow page.

- **Mocha.** White text against a light brown backdrop.

- **Sepia.** Black text against a yellow-brown page. See Figure 4-14.

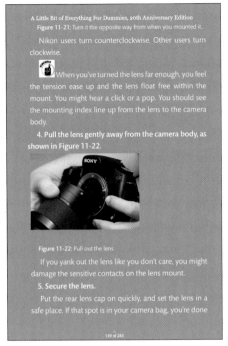

A Little Bit of Everything For Dummies, 20th Anniversary Edition

Figure 11-21: Turn it the opposite way from when you mounted it.

Nikon users turn counterclockwise. Other users turn clockwise.

When you've turned the lens far enough, you feel the tension ease up and the lens float free within the mount. You might hear a click or a pop. You should see the mounting index line up from the lens to the camera body.

4. Pull the lens gently away from the camera body, as shown in Figure 11-22.

Figure 11-22: Pull out the lens

If you yank out the lens like you don't care, you might damage the sensitive contacts on the lens mount.

5. Secure the lens.

Put the rear lens cap on quickly, and set the lens in a safe place. If that spot is in your camera bag, you're done

139 of 283

Figure 4-14: Changing the theme may improve visibility in very dark or very bright light.

Publisher Defaults

Maybe you want to leave all of the decisionmaking to a professional graphic designer. Drag the switch to On to use the formatting recommended by the publisher; you'll see the selections on the menu, but all other options will be unavailable.

Reading a Magazine

Magazines come in all shapes, sizes, and special designs. Their electronic formats vary greatly; the way you see pages from a periodical using the NOOK HD or HD+ may be different from one magazine to another, and some may have interactive features.

Most magazines offer two views. You get to choose:

- ✓ **Page view** shows the entire page, including text and images. See Figure 4-15.

- ✓ **Article view** shows text only.

Figure 4-15: Try Page view in a spectacular magazine like *National Geographic.*

Page view

This digital representation of the printed magazine has photographs, drawings, charts, and other elements. You'll see small images in the lower half of the screen. Page view is available in both portrait and landscape modes.

- ✓ To move through the magazine, swipe your finger along the thumbnail images.

- ✓ Tap a page to jump directly to it; a progress bar below the images shows where you are in the entire issue.

- ✓ As you read a page, tap the right side of the screen to move to the next page; tap the left side to go back a page.

  Why is navigating a magazine different than navigating a book? Good question. Magazine publishers use a different electronic design than book publishers.

- ✓ To make the thumbnail images reappear, tap in the middle of the screen.

Article view

This format shows articles with few (or no) illustrations or photos. You can scroll through the text as you would in a book. See Figure 4-16.

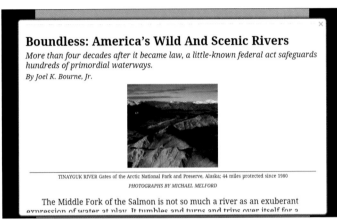

Boundless: America's Wild And Scenic Rivers

More than four decades after it became law, a little-known federal act safeguards hundreds of primordial waterways.

By Joel K. Bourne, Jr.

TINAYGUK RIVER Gates of the Arctic National Park and Preserve, Alaska; 44 miles protected since 1980

PHOTOGRAPHS BY MICHAEL MELFORD

The Middle Fork of the Salmon is not so much a river as an exuberant expression of water at play. It tumbles and turns and trips over itself for a

Figure 4-16: Article view emphasizes the text of a magazine piece; you can always go back to page view to enjoy photographs and illustrations.

You can also go directly from article to article:

1. **Tap the center of the screen.**
2. **Tap the Content icon at the bottom of the page.**

   A window opens.

3. **Tap the cover, table of contents, or specific article.**

Reading a Newspaper

Whether you've downloaded a single issue or you subscribe, newspapers are on your Daily Shelf and on the Newsstand page of your Library.

✔ To open a newspaper, tap its front page. When it opens, the front page shows headlines and one or two paragraphs from the start of major articles.

✔ To read an article in more depth, tap its headline or the introductory paragraphs.

✔ To share parts of an article, tap in the middle of the page. From the reading tools, choose Share or Notes (if the publisher has allowed those features).

✔ Bookmark a page by tapping in the upper-right corner of the page.

✔ To turn to the next page of a newspaper, do any of the following:

- Tap along the right edge of the screen.

- Swipe your finger from right to left across the screen.

- Swipe your finger from low to high on the screen.

✔ To go back a page in a newspaper, do one of these actions:

- Tap along the left edge of the screen.

- Swipe your finger from left to right across the screen.

- Swipe your finger from high to low on the screen.

Reading for Kids of All Ages

The NOOK HD or HD+ offers some special features for young readers (and those of us who sit by their side as they discover the joys of reading) with special features that are part of the NOOK Kids picture books. Some children's books have a bit of animation that you can set into motion by tapping the screen; others read aloud parts of the book. See Figure 4-17.

Children's books open in landscape mode to better present the two-page spreads of most picture books. You may find the speaker tough to hear in noisy situations; one solution is to use *two* sets of earphones plugged into a simple splitter attached to the tablet's audio output. Splitters are available at most electronics stores and shacks.

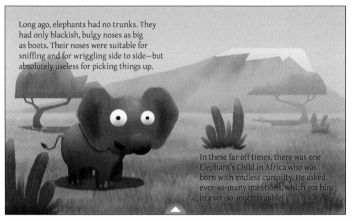

Long ago, elephants had no trunks. They had only blackish, bulgy noses as big as boots. Their noses were suitable for sniffing and for wriggling side to side—but absolutely useless for picking things up.

In these far off times, there was one Elephant's Child in Africa who was born with endless curiosity. He asked ever-so-many questions, which got him in ever-so-much trouble!

Figure 4-17: A book for kids of all ages.

Manipulate with these tips, too:

- ✔ To make text bigger, double-tap it to enlarge it. Double-tap to return to the original size and position.
- ✔ To make text bigger, zoom in by pinching in on the image and text.
- ✔ Drag an image to move it around on the page.

Moving from page to page

Follow these steps:

- ✔ Swipe to the left (drag your finger from right to left across the screen) to go forward.
- ✔ Tap anywhere on the right edge of the screen.
- ✔ To go backward in the book, swipe to the right or tap the left side.

Skipping part of a children's book

To go from one part of a kid's book to another, follow these steps:

1. **Tap the white arrow at the bottom of the screen.**

   Small pages from the book appear.

2. **Slide your finger across the images.**

3. **Tap the small image of the page you want to read.**

Choosing a reading style

Some children's books can narrate. Others move. These special features appear only if the book includes them. See Figure 4-18.

Figure 4-18: Some NOOK Kids books include prerecorded audio tracks, or you may be able to add your own.

Read by Myself

Just the words and pictures. Tap the blue button to open the book. Some special activities may be marked with a white star; tap the star to play. Better yet, let a kid tap the star.

Read to Me or Read and Play

Read and Play books have audio tracks, and interactive features, marked with a white star. Tap the orange Read to Me, or the purple Read and Play buttons to hear the author or an actor read aloud.

If you're enjoying a Read and Play book, you can only turn the pages by tapping the onscreen arrows. The pages won't turn if you tap them.

Read and Record

Daddy or Mommy (or a child!) can become the voice of a book. Here's how:

1. **Tap the cover of a kid's book that has the Read and Record feature.**

2. **On the opening screen, tap the green Read and Record button.**

   The book opens to the first page.

3. **Tap the green Read and Record button.**

   It will change to a Stop button. But don't stop.

4. **Start reading.**

   Here are some tips:

   - The tiny hole on the top side of the NOOK HD or HD+ is the microphone. Don't cover it with your hand while you're recording.

   - Hold the tablet about 15 inches away from your mouth.

   - Try to record in a quiet place without background noise.

5. **When you're done recording, tap the Stop button.**

Keep these general recording tips in mind:

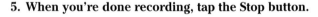
If you'd like to hear your recording right away, press the Play button. Press the Pause button when you're done listening.

If you're a perfectionist (or if someone dropped a pile of plates while the microphone was on), press the Re-record button to do it again.

To keep recording, swipe or tap to the next page and then tap the Record button.

> ✔ To end a recording session at any time, tap the Done button in the lower left. A screen asks you to choose a picture as a symbol. Type a name for the recording.

> ✔ To play a recording, open the book and tap the picture icon for the file you created.

> ✔ To re-record, change the name, or delete the audio file, tap the Edit button next to the picture icon and then choose the option you want.

The recording you make is saved in the My Files folder; they aren't part of the NOOK Kids book itself. When you connect your NOOK HD or HD+ to a desktop or laptop computer, you can make a copy of the file there, or move it to the microSD memory card you may have installed in the tablet.

Studying a NOOK Comics Book

Pow! Oomph! Wow! The NOOK HD or HD+ can display specially formatted NOOK comics in portrait or landscape mode. Moving within a NOOK Comics book is very similar to the steps involved in NOOK Kids titles.

> ✔ Tap the cover of a comic book to open it. See Figure 4-19.

> ✔ Swipe left or right to go forward or back, or tap the right or left side of the page for the same effect.

> ✔ Tap in the center of the screen to bring up the reader tools, including small versions of the entire document. Tap any image to go directly to a particular page.

> ✔ To zoom in on text and images, double-tap or use the pinch-out gesture. Double-tap again to return the page to normal.

> ✔ Bookmark a page by tapping the + icon in the upper right. Once you place a marker, tap the center of the page to display reader tools, tap the Content icon, and then tap the Bookmarks tab.

> ✔ Jump directly to any bookmarked page by tapping the bookmark.

Figure 4-19: Betty and Veronica never looked so good as they do in NOOK comics.

Flipping Through Catalogs

Newly arrived with the NOOK HD or HD+: colorful catalogs from some of the nation's leading retailers. They're all free (the catalogs, that is), which saves trees and postage. You can get a single issue, or subscribe to the catalogs and get them as they're produced. They're available through the NOOK Shop, and I describe the subscription process in Chapter 5.

You flip through the pages of a catalog just as you do through a magazine. I especially like using the page curl animation as I hunt for an especially sturdy pair of hiking boots; I'm in training for an expedition from my office to the harbor, a hike of just under a mile that includes a dirt road, a stretch of gravel and, eventually, cobblestones.

Knowing Your PDF from Your EPUB

Before you start worrying about file format, here's the deal: If you buy or download a book or other publication from the

Barnes & Noble online store, it will work on your NOOK HD or HD+. And the same should apply to any other major online bookseller or free source (like the Gutenberg Project at www. gutenberg.org).

Remember: I'm talking about books here. Your NOOK HD or HD+ can also display word processing, spreadsheet, presentation, and other files. And I show you how to create your own EPUB and PDF files as well. But not in this chapter; that happens in Chapter 5.

Both EPUB and PDF file types come in two types: protected and unprotected. A *protected* book has *digital rights management (DRM)* restrictions. Basically, there's some limit on whether (or how often) you can copy, lend, or transfer the title. Nearly every professional author and publisher supports the concept of DRM. Please don't attempt to pick a fight with me about this: Authors need to pay their mortgage and put food on the table, just like you.

EPUB

If you have a choice, go for an EPUB e-book file so that you have the widest variety of customization and special features.

EPUBs are free and open (meaning that anyone can produce and distribute a file using this standard). That doesn't mean you can release a document based on copyrighted material that belongs to someone else. An EPUB file is also reflowable, meaning you can change font, font size, and other things.

PDF

PDFs can be created in two different forms. More advanced PDFs can include fonts and images, and will let you enlarge pages. However, some PDFs are scans (think of them as snapshots), like the one shown in Figure 4-20. They may look fine on your NOOK, or you may need to adjust the zoom and move around on each individual page to read the text. And these most primitive of e-books don't allow you to change font or size and don't link to the web.

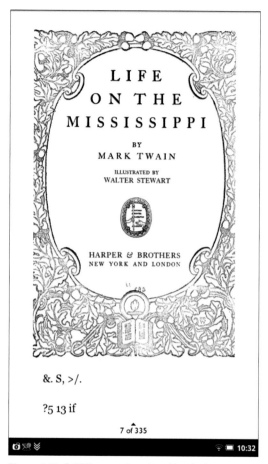

Figure 4-20: A PDF scan of a printed book gives you a set of pictures of pages rather than reflowable, searchable text.

Side Loading Files

You can download files over the Internet via your Wi-Fi connection from your NOOK to a wireless router. But you can also bring files to a NOOK HD or HD+ by side loading, too. *Side loading* means moving a copy of a file from your laptop or personal computer to your NOOK using the USB cable that comes with the device (or an identical replacement cable).

Use only the USB cable provided with your NOOK HD or HD+ or an exact duplicate. There are many different types of USB cables and using the wrong one could damage the physical connector and cause tablet troubles.

What kind of files can you side load onto a NOOK HD or HD+? There are two answers, so I'll give you both:

✔ You can store any compatible audio, video, picture, text, spreadsheet, presentation, or book file on your NOOK and use it to play them back. The NOOK can read the following file types:

- **EPUB.** The default format for books.

- **PDF.** Another format used for some books and publications, and for things like catalogs, instruction manuals, and documents.

- **Word.** Microsoft Office text files in doc, docx, docm, dot, dotx, and dotm formats.

- **Excel.** Microsoft Office spreadsheet files in xls, xlsx, xlsm, xlt, xltx, and xltm formats.

- **PowerPoint.** Microsoft Office presentation files in ppt, pptx, pptm, pps, ppsx, ppsm, pot, potx, and potm formats. (Special effects including animations, transitions, and multi-image slides will not show those features on the tablet.) See Figure 4-21.

- **Plain text.** Unformatted text from many sources, stored as a txt file.

- **Web pages.** Material stored using HTML, stored as htm, html, or xhtml files.

- **Comic book archive.** One great leap for man (and womankind): an advanced scheme for comic books, stored using the cbz format.

- **Music, video, and image files.** You know of what I speak.

- **Music and audio.** The NOOK HD or HD+ can play files in any of these formats: aac, amr, mid, midi, mp3, m4a, ogg, or wav.

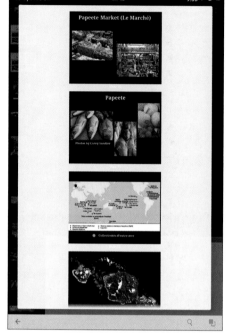

Figure 4-21: You can work with basic PowerPoint functions; advanced animations and transitions are not supported.

- **Video.** The tablet can play media files as large as 2GB, in any of these formats: Adobe Flash, 3gp, 3g2, mkv, mp4, or m4v.

- **Images.** The preferred format is jpg.

✔ You can place any kind of electronic file — including formats that won't work on the tablet— as if the tablet were an external hard drive. I sometimes do exactly that, storing files I may need on a business trip, with the expectation of side loading them onto a desktop or laptop computer if I need to use them.

As delivered, the NOOK HD or HD+ can open and display or play any of the file formats I have listed. The facility, though, is read-only; you can't edit or change them. However, you can buy apps through www.BN.com that let you do some basic Microsoft Office editing.

Always keep backup copies of important files on your personal computer. That's true even if you use your NOOK as a backup device for some of your files when you travel. For example, if you're traveling to give a presentation, you can store copies of PowerPoint and Word files on the device as a second copy in case your laptop fails or disappears.

Moving files from a computer to your NOOK

To transfer files from your personal computer to your NOOK, do this:

1. **Turn on your Windows-based or Macintosh personal computer and allow it to fully load the operating system.**

2. **Turn on your NOOK.**

   It's faster to the starting line than a big computer, but then again, it's not a big computer.

3. **Connect the 30-pin connector end of the USB cable that came with your NOOK to the tablet.**

4. **Connect the rectangular end of the USB cable to a USB port on your personal computer.**

   After a few moments, your computer should say it has detected a new disk drive. Depending on your computer, the drive may show up identified by name or by model number, or it may just be listed as an extra drive. (On my computer, my NOOK HD+ shows up as BNTV600, which is its model number.) A second entry is for the microSD/SDHC memory slot. If your computer has one internal hard drive plus a CD/DVD drive, the built-in internal storage of the NOOK may show up as Removable Disk E and Removable Drive F.

   Some Windows computers may ask if you want to install a driver for a NOOK device. Click Cancel to close this dialog box.

   • If your PC uses Windows XP, you need Windows Media Player 11 or later for your computer to recognize your NOOK. That software is available for free from Microsoft; it is usually installed as part of automatic updates.

- If you use a Mac computer, the first time you connect your NOOK, you'll see a NOOK drive on your computer monitor. The drive will have a file called MyNOOK Setup. Double-click the file and follow the onscreen instructions. This is one-time installation.

5. **On your computer, click the NOOK drive to open it.**

   Unless advised a technician tells you otherwise, I suggest you consider opening only two folders: My Files or Pictures.

6. **Click My Files to open that subfolder.**

7. **Drag and drop files from the computer to the right subfolder.**

   Here are the folders on the NOOK HD or HD+ tablet:

   - Books
   - Documents
   - Magazines
   - Music
   - My Downloads
   - Newspapers
   - NOOK Kids Recordings
   - Pictures
   - Videos
   - Wallpapers

In most cases, it doesn't matter where you place a particular type of file because the NOOK will sort it out for you. Files in picture format will appear in the gallery; videos will appear in the video player. But it does make your NOOK nicely organized. And one more thing: You can create your own folder on the tablet, using the Make Folder (or equivalent) command on your computer, and use it to store files of your choice.

Preparing files for the NOOK

What if you have files on your desktop or laptop computer that you want to use on your NOOK HD or HD+, but the files are stored in the wrong format? In most cases, you can use a program or utility on your computer to convert the files to a compatible format.

For example, any file you can open in Microsoft Office can be saved in one of the formats that the NOOK can display; just use the Save As command and select the proper format. The same process can be used to convert photos or drawings to JPG format, using a graphics program such as Adobe Photoshop, Adobe Photoshop Elements, or a Macintosh image editor.

When you process an image for the NOOK HD or HD+, consider resizing it. Set the image to about 4 x 6 inches. The resolution can be set at 72 or 96 dpi. Choose Save As, select JPG, and type a new name. That way you don't lose the original larger, higher-resolution file.

Knowing what file types work

The NOOK HD and HD+ can display files saved in a wide range of file formats. Two caveats here, though:

- ✔ Not every type of file will look as great as those that have been created using one of the preferred formats.

- ✔ You can't *edit* a file on the NOOK without adding special apps for that purpose.

Here are the supported file formats for both devices:

- ✔ **E-books:** EPUB (B&N DRM, Adobe DRM, and non-DRM files), PDF, CBZ, ePIB

- ✔ **Other documents:** DRP, FOLIO, OFIP, TXT, RTF, LOG, CSV, EML, ZIP

- ✔ **Microsoft Office documents:** DOC, DOCX, XLS, XLSX, PPT, PPS, PPSX, PPTX

- ✔ **Music and audio:** MP3, MP4, M4A, WAV, AAC, MIDI, AMR, OGG, FLAC (Audio codecs: MP3, AAC [ADTS], AMR, LPCM, OGG Vorbis)

- ✔ **Video:** MP4, M4V, 3GP, MKV, WEBM (Video codecs: H.264, MPEG-4, H.263, VP8)

- ✔ **Pictures or photos:** JPEG, JPG, GIF, PNG, BMP

The NOOK HD and HD+ include an app called OfficeSuite that allows you to view most files created with Microsoft Office software, including Word, Excel, and PowerPoint. If you want to perform basic editing on these files, you can buy the OfficeSuite Pro app in the NOOK Shop.

Ejecting the NOOK from a computer

When you connect your NOOK to a laptop or desktop computer, the device becomes the equivalent of an extra hard disk drive — extra storage. To protect against damaging the files that you copy to the tablet, you should *eject* the device before you physically unplug the USB cable. (The official instructions say this is a "must do." I classify it as a "should do." In any case, I know I do do that old voodoo that I do so well, because a corrupted file is not pretty.)

You can eject the NOOK by

✔ Clicking the Eject button. (You might see instructions onscreen.)

✔ Using the operating system (described in the following sections).

Windows-based computer or laptop

Follow these steps:

1. **Open the My Computer (or Computer) folder.**

2. **Click the icon for the Removable Drive for the NOOK.**

   Click it just once with the left mouse button.

3. **Right-click the Removable Drive icon.**

   A submenu appears.

4. **Click Eject.**

5. **If a microSD card is in your NOOK, repeat Steps 1-4.**

6. **Unplug the USB cable from the computer.**

   You can unplug the cable from the tablet or leave it attached if you'll connect again to the computer soon.

After the tablet is ejected and you remove the USB cable from the computer, the tablet tells you that it's processing any new files. Give it a moment to put books and documents on the shelf.

Here is a second way to eject a NOOK from a Windows-based machine:

1. **On the taskbar at the bottom of the Windows screen, click the Safely Remove Hardware icon.**

   You should see something like, "Safely remove USB mass storage device- Drive x."

2. **Choose based on your situation:**

   - If only one device is attached, then this is your NOOK tablet. Go to Step 3.

   - If more than one device is attached, choose the drive letter assigned to the NOOK.

3. **Click the item in the pop-up notice.**

   The system should respond with "Safe to remove hardware."

4. **If a microSD card is in your NOOK, repeat Steps 1-3.**

5. **Unplug the USB cable from the computer.**

   You can also unplug the cable from the tablet or leave it attached if you intend to connect again to the computer soon.

Macintosh computer or laptop

Follow these steps:

1. **Open the Finder and select the drive for the NOOK.**

2. **From the File menu, select Eject.**

3. **If a microSD card is in your NOOK, eject that memory card.**

4. **Unplug the USB cable from the computer.**

   You can also unplug the cable from the reader or leave it attached if you intend to connect again to the computer soon.

Traveling Abroad with a NOOK

Nothing prevents you from taking your NOOK outside of the United States, although some roadblocks keep you from buying something when you're in another country. Why? Because most publisher-author contracts restrict selling a book in foreign countries (or indicate varying royalty rates).

Here's a guide to the international lay of the land:

- ✔ You can read anything that's already on your NOOK as you travel anywhere in the world.

- ✔ As of the end of 2012, the NOOK HD and HD+ were for sale only in the United States and the United Kingdom; more countries will be added.

- ✔ You can only buy content for your tablet if you have a billing address in the United States or the United Kingdom. Purchases can be made anywhere in the world.

- ✔ You can download items you've already bought from anywhere in the world where you can obtain a Wi-Fi signal.

- ✔ You can lend and borrow e-books from anywhere in the world.

- ✔ Periodicals are automatically downloaded to your NOOK anywhere you can connect to a Wi-Fi system.

- ✔ The NOOK HD or HD+, as first delivered, uses either American or British English; other character sets will be available when the devices are being sold elsewhere.

Oh, and one more thing: The battery recharger for your NOOK has prongs that connect to wall outlets in the United States and Canada. It *can* work with power from about 110 to 240 volts. You need a plug adapter if you want to use the NOOK HD or HD+ in a country that uses plugs of other shapes. You *don't* need to convert or reduce the voltage — just change the shape of the plug.

Chapter 5

Stocking Shelves and Adding Apps

In This Chapter

▶ Going to the NOOK Shop

▶ Using password security

▶ Buying things to read and use

▶ Storing your back shelves in the NOOK Cloud

▶ Loaning and borrowing books

*M*an and woman cannot live on bread alone. They also need great books. It is simply unacceptable to own a handsome and technologically astounding device like a NOOK HD or HD+ and not have it stocked with books, magazines, catalogs, newspapers, and the occasional comic book.

In this chapter you explore ways to fill your electronic tablet with bestsellers, literary classics, dozens of *For Dummies* books, and obscure research material of interest only to you. I will also tell you how to find free e-books. You also read about how to download apps to expand the capabilities of your NOOK HD or HD+.

For most of this chapter, I talk about Barnes & Noble and the NOOK Shop because they separately and jointly are the main seller of the NOOK devices and because you can easily get to their online store by tapping the Shop icon on your tablet. However, nearly all of the other online booksellers are similar.

Welcome B&N Shoppers!

The first time you turn on your NOOK HD or HD+, before you can do anything other than admire its handsome design, you've got to accept the terms dictated by a lawyer for the other side, and you've got to register it with the authorities: Barnes & Noble.

And before you can register, you've got to connect to a Wi-Fi system and, through it, to the Internet.

 What if you don't have Wi-Fi service? If you buy your NOOK HD or HD+ at a Barnes & Noble store, you can register the device right there; all NOOK owners are entitled to use the free Wi-Fi service any time they're in one of the stores.

If you buy your NOOK and have it shipped to you, you can take it to a Barnes & Noble store or a public library or other location that offers Wi-Fi service.

Here are the steps to register your NOOK and get it ready for use:

1. **Attach the supplied USB cable to the NOOK HD or HD+.**

   The larger 30-pin cable connects to the NOOK and only fits in one orientation.

2. **Connect the other end of the USB cable into the AC adapter.**

3. **Plug the AC adapter into a source of power.**

   Depending on how long it's been since your NOOK left the factory in no-longer-exotic China, the battery may have enough juice to allow you to register the device while it charges. If you see a message onscreen that the battery is empty, you'll have to wait perhaps an hour or two until it has enough power.

4. **Select your country of residence.**

5. **Connect to a Wi-Fi network.**

   If you're working from home or your office, choose the right network and enter your username and password.

6. **Select your location and time zone.**

7. **Read the terms of service and tap Agree.**

   You've no other choice; you *have* to accept them to use the NOOK HD or HD+. There's nothing out of the ordinary in the terms, other than turning over the key to your house and the technical specs for the gravity-free hovercraft you've just designed. It's all in there, except for the part about the house and the hovercraft.

   You can also create a B&N account from your personal computer ahead of time. Then all you need is your username and password to enter when you set it up. You can do so from `www.BN.com` or `www.barnesandnoble.com` or `www.nook.com`. They all go to the same place.

8. **Either link your NOOK to an existing Barnes & Noble account or create a new one.**

   - **If you already have a NOOK account:** Tap Yes, I Have an Account. Then enter the email address and password for your account. Tap Submit. If you already have an account, this allows your tablet to retrieve any e-books and periodicals already in your account.

   - **If you don't have a NOOK account:** Tap No, I Need to Create an Account. Then tap the Create an Account button. Fill in the form with your name, email, a password, and other information as requested. Tap Submit.

   Your NOOK is now linked to an account.

9. **Follow the onscreen instructions to set up your primary profile.**

   Based on the choices you make you will receive some free samples and suggestions of items you might like to purchase. See Figure 5-1.

In addition to the e-reader on the NOOK HD or HD+, Barnes & Noble also offers free software that lets you read (and buy) publications on devices including desktop and laptop PCs, Macintoshes, iPads, iPhones, and various Android devices.

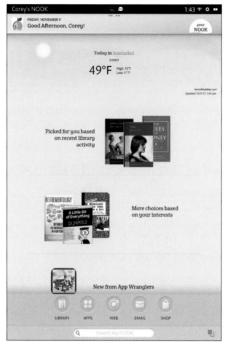

Figure 5-1: After you registering and indicating your interests, your device will offer a changing set of customized recommendations, called Your NOOK Today.

Locking Things Down

Please allow me to ask a few questions:

- ✔ Will you ever loan your NOOK HD or HD+ to someone else?

- ✔ Will anyone (family, friends, acquaintances, or perfect strangers) ever have access to your NOOK when you're not around?

- ✔ Can you conceive the possibility that your NOOK might someday (perish the thought) be lost or stolen?

If the answer to any of these questions is Yes or Maybe, I recommend creating a password and making anyone who's going to buy something enter that password. Make it a pretty tough password, too. The best password is so complex and unobvious that no one can guess it. My favorite type of password is a phone number or an address that has no direct connection to you but which you can recall from memory. Oh, and don't write it down on a sticky note applied to the bottom of the NOOK itself.

To make sure someone (you included) has to enter a password before buying something on your NOOK, follow these steps:

1. **Press the ∩ button to go to the Home screen.**

2. **Within the status bar, tap the settings (gear) icon.**

3. **Tap All Settings.**

4. **Tap Applications in the category list on the left.**

5. **Tap Shop in the list on the right.**

6. **Tap in the check box beside Password Protect Purchases for Adult Profiles.**

   If the check box is bold, rather than gray (see Figure 5-2), the option is already turned on; you don't need to tap it.

7. **In the dialog box that appears, use the keyboard to enter your B&N account password.**

8. **Tap OK.**

   From now on, you'll need to enter your Shop password before buying anything.

If you decide you want to *remove* the requirement for entry of the password, follow Steps 1-4, then do this:

1. **Tap in the check box to remove the marker**

   You're asked to enter the password one more time.

2. **Enter the password.**

3. **Tap OK to complete the process.**

Figure 5-2: Requiring a password for all purchases protects you against unauthorized shopping from your NOOK.

Shopping from Your NOOK

The bottom line, of course, is that without books, magazines, videos, music, apps, or document files, your NOOK Tablet is simply a fancy paperweight. You're going to want to fill it up. See Figure 5-3.

Here's how to shop in the B&N Store:

1. **Press the ∩ button to see the nav buttons.**
2. **Tap the Shop button.**

You will arrive at the section of the NOOK Shop you last visited. If you want to go to the front page, tap the home icon in the upper-left corner; appropriately, it looks like a little house. Just as you do when you walk into a brick-and-mortar bookstore, you have to make your way past promotions for new titles and specials. What you see today is likely to be different from what you saw yesterday or will find tomorrow. Here are some typical offerings for browsing:

- **Books.** Choose from romance, mystery, crime, science fiction, biography, memoir, business and personal finance, history, humor . . . think of it as strolling the aisles of a store. Also included in the book department: comics.

- **Magazines.** Choose *Cosmopolitan* to *Maxim,* from *National Geographic* to *Southern Living*, from *Bon Appetit* to *Fitness Magazine.* In most cases, you can buy one issue or subscribe.

Figure 5-3: The front page of the NOOK Shop is a cornucopia of books, periodicals, videos, apps, and other types of reading material.

✔ **Movies & TV.** Watch this space, plus other enhancements to the NOOK HD and HD+ operating system, as Barnes & Noble rolls out its new NOOK Video service. In the initial release, you could buy or rent movies and tv shows from a pretty limited selection. See Figure 5-4.

If you select the *streaming* option, you can begin watching immediately, although the quality might be affected by your current Wi-Fi signal strength. The other option is to download the movie, so you can watch it once it has fully arrived. Renting gives you 30 days to begin watching; once you start playing it, you have 24 hours to finish. When you reach the closing credits, your right to view ends. Buying a video gives you unlimited rights to view it over and over and over.

✔ **Kids.** Several hundred books (picture and chapter) are there for pre-readers through teens. Included are Read and Play Books, which add narration, sound effects, and interactive features. Chapter 3 tells more about kids' books.

Figure 5-4: The NOOK Video service offers sale, rental, or streaming view of movies, television shows, and special features.

✔ **Apps.** A growing selection of small programs (apps) is what you find here, "curated" by Barnes & Noble from the broader selection that's been developed for Android-based devices. B&N says it wants to concentrate on book-related apps as well as carefully selected games and utilities for people on the go.

✔ **Newspapers.** Choose from *The New York Times, Financial Times,* and *The Onion.* You'll find not just national papers but also regional publications and a handful of international newspapers. See Figure 5-5.

✔ **Catalogs.** Here's something completely different, in addition to being pretty nifty. With the debut of the NOOK HD and HD+, the NOOK Shop began offering several dozen catalogs at a great price: free. They're beautifully presented and easy to view — especially on the larger HD+ screen. The first round of catalogs were mostly clothing, and mostly for women; I expect other online sellers will begin to convert their periodicals for this purpose.

Figure 5-5: More newspapers are publishing electronic editions that they automatically deliver to subscribers.

In addition, you can go through Popular Lists to find things like the B&N Top 100, *The New York Times* bestsellers, and new releases. Again, these lists change over time and include things like seasonal specials (Christmas, Mother's Day, Father's Day, and the like). Tap any of the lists to explore. To read more about a suggestion, double-tap the cover.

Searching for a specific book

As much as I love to browse the aisles (physical or electronic) of a good bookstore, sometimes I know exactly what I want. See Figure 5-6.

Figure 5-6: You can search by author name, subject, or title. The NOOK Shop shows a customized display of available titles and those you can pre-order.

To search for a particular book or periodical:

1. **Tap the Search Shop field at the bottom of the Shop screen.**

   The virtual onscreen keyboard appears.

2. **Type the title, author, or subject you're looking for.**

   You don't have to distinguish between a title, author, or subject. The search engine will sort through all of the possibilities.

3. **Tap the search icon (magnifying glass) on the keyboard.**

   Scroll through the results by dragging your finger up or down. A blue banner shows the prices on the B&N site. If you see a gray Purchased label, you already bought that title for the current account; once you've paid, you can always download it again.

Buying a book

Find a book you want. Here's what else to do:

1. **Tap the cover to see its details.**

   Sometimes you can see a sample from the book — an entire chapter or a hop, skip, and jump through the pages. See Figure 5-7.

   Tap the Share button to tell people what you've found. (Perhaps you'd like to drop a hint about the perfect birthday gift for you?) You can rate and review your thoughts about the title, posting them to Facebook or Twitter.

2. **Tap the blue box that shows the price.**

   The button will change to say Confirm.

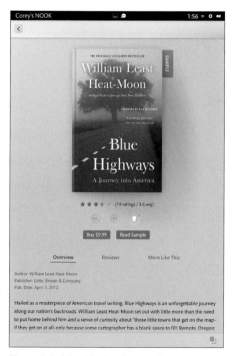

Figure 5-7: A book's details page lets you access a sample (in some books) and the all-important blue Buy button.

Many publishers let you download a sample of a book; it's sort of like flipping through the pages of a print volume at a bookstore. Once you're done with the sample, you can buy the whole thing.

3. Tap the Confirm button.

Your credit card is charged; the book starts coming to your tablet; a progress bar shows you how much has arrived. (If a download is interrupted because of a problem with the wireless connection or other causes, it will automatically resume the next time it gets a chance.) The new item appears on the Active Shelf on the Home screen and in your Library. And it wears a New badge until you open it.

If you're asking to download a copy of a free book at the Barnes & Noble store, you still go through the "purchase" process; the cost will register as $0. If you pre-order an e-book, you're charged when it's officially published.

Buying magazines or newspapers

You can buy individual issues of a newspaper or magazine, or subscribe to daily, weekly, or monthly delivery of the periodical. Just as in the world of paper and ink, the best deals come with longer-term subscriptions. Once you buy, the first issue downloads immediately. See Figure 5-8.

Nearly every magazine and newspaper offers free 14-day trials; you can get one free trial for each publication. If you cancel the subscription before the end of the trial, your credit card isn't charged. Otherwise, deliveries continue and your credit card is charged automatically at the monthly subscription rate. To cancel a periodical subscription, go to your account at www.BN.com, log in, and go to the Manage Subscriptions section.

Buying a single issue

To buy a single issue, follow these steps:

1. Tap the cover to reveal the Details page.

You'll see the price for the current issue, and elsewhere on the page you can see the price for a monthly subscription.

2. **To buy just the latest issue, tap the Buy Current Issue button.**

   To buy a subscription, tap Free Trial.

   If you subscribe, you get the first issue and have 14 days to decide whether you to continue. If you cancel within those 14 days, you'll have received that first issue for free. If you *don't* cancel, you're on the hook for at least one month at the subscription price — but you can cancel any time.

   It's almost a no-brainer: Take the free trial for any magazine or newspaper you want to try. The month-to-month subscription usually represents a significant savings over buying a single issue, and you can cancel at any time. Note that you can only take a free trial once for any particular publication.

Figure 5-8: The magazines in the NOOK Shop include most major news, fashion, self-help, and special interest titles.

3. Tap Confirm.

The issue downloads.

4. Tap the Read button.

Subscribing to a periodical

The subscription process begins with a free trial; if you don't cancel before the end of the trial, you are automatically subscribed. See Figure 5-9.

1. Tap the cover and open the Details page.

2. Tap the Free Trial button.

3. Tap Confirm.

4. Tap the Start My Free Trial button.

You can always return to the Shop page by tapping the Shop icon in the upper-left corner of the screen.

Confirm Your Order

You are about to begin your 14 day FREE TRIAL subscription to: Popular Science
$1.99 per month plus applicable taxes

After the trial, you will be charged monthly at the then-current subscription rate unless you cancel at myNOOK.com.

Free Trial Terms

Cancel   Start My Free Trial

Figure 5-9: Accepting a free trial subscription to a magazine or newspaper allows you 14 days to decide, and generally offers a better rate than buying individual issues.

Subscribing to catalogs

Catalogs are free; the companies that provide them very much want you salivating over their shoes, dresses, fruitcakes, and gadgets. Some of the first offerings are from major sellers like L.L. Bean, Sharper Image, Omaha Steaks, Pottery Barn, and Ross-Simons.

When you tap the cover of a catalog, you wind up on a purchase screen very much like one for a magazine. See Figure 5-10. You'll see two choices, and both are free:

✔ **Current Edition:** Just this once.

✔ **Free Subscription:** You're going to get each new edition of the catalog.

I'm not going too far out on a limb to predict that eventually you will be able to directly order items by tapping on them in the catalogs. A few companies already have links from a product number to a web-based order form, and some catalogs have links to video demonstrations and other bells and whistles.

Figure 5-10: It's tough to resist electronically thumbing through the handsome pages of a catalog on the NOOK HD or HD+.

Paying the bill

Unless you say otherwise, your credit card is charged when you buy something from Barnes & Noble. It's all done for you; there are no receipts to sign.

If you have a Barnes & Noble gift card, you can add its value to your account. I discuss this process early in Chapter 2.

Here's a recap: The eGift card is used before your credit card is charged. Here's how to associate a gift card with your account:

1. **Press the ∩ button to display the Home screen.**

2. **Tap the Settings gear icon in the status bar at the top of the screen.**

3. **Tap All Settings.**

4. **Tap Applications in the category list on the left.**

5. **Tap Shop in the settings panel on the right.**

6. **Tap Gift Cards.**

7. **Tap Add Gift Card.**

8. **Type the identifying number for the gift card or certificate.**

9. **Type the PIN from the card.**

You can register three gift cards, eGift cards, and online gift certificates at any one time. If you have more than that in your wallet, enter them after you've spent the others. When in doubt, call Barnes & Noble customer service for help.

Buying apps from B&N

The NOOK Tablet can accept new programs that teach it new tricks: apps. An *app* (short for application) is a small software program. Where do you get apps? Well, in the case of the NOOK Tablet, www.BN.com is the only official source. See Figure 5-11.

Although the selection of apps offered through the NOOK Shop has grown steadily, B&N is steadfast in its focus on the reading experience. At the end of 2012, there is no Skype for online phone calls, no online banking, no direct access to books sold by other companies. Some utilities allow basic editing of Microsoft Office files, a few calendar and email utilities, some cute games, and a selection of calendar and travel apps. And, of course, because the NOOK HD and HD+ don't have a built-in camera, you'll find just a few utilities related to photography or moviemaking.

Figure 5-11: Apps extend and enhance the capabilities of the NOOK.

Here's how to buy an app:

1. **Press the ∩ button to display the Home screen.**

2. **Tap Shop in the nav buttons.**

   You'll find yourself on the last section of the shop you visited.

3. **In the Browse section, tap Apps.**

   Look at categories (Education & Reference, Games, Entertainment, Productivity, Tools & Utilities, Social, or News and Weather) or tap in the Search bar at the bottom of the screen and hunt for what you're looking for.

Tap the name of an app to find out more details.

4. Tap the blue Buy button, which also displays the price.

You get to tap the Free button if it doesn't cost anything.

The file downloads to your tablet. If there's an interruption, the downloading starts back up when your Wi-Fi is working properly. Apps will show up in your Library and on the Recent Shelf on the Home screen. See Figure 5-12.

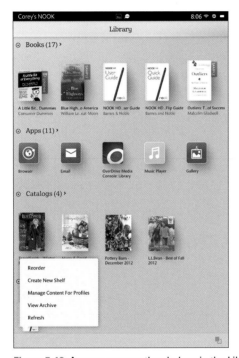

Figure 5-12: Apps appear on the shelves in the Library, and you can get to them by tapping Apps in the nav buttons section of the Home screen.

You can shop for apps from your desktop or laptop computer, or directly from a NOOK HD or HD+ when any of these devices are connected to the Internet. Anything you buy (or free apps) are included in your account; the next time you use your NOOK HD or HD+, you'll see the apps on the home screen with a Download badge. Tap the apps and they'll get to your tablet.

You could download and use apps developed for the full Android community, even if they're not approved by Barnes & Noble. Because the NOOK HD, HD+, and earlier versions including the NOOK Tablet and NOOKcolor use a variation of the Android operating system, several developers and hackers have found ways to change the way the device acts.

Two maneuvers exist: One is to actually change the operating system within the NOOK; that works, but it violates the terms of service to which you agreed when you first registered the device. (Remember the legal notice?) If you run into problems with an altered operating system and can't reset the system back to the way it arrived from the factory, *your warranty probably isn't going to be honored.*

The other way is to add an alternate version of the operating system that is installed from the microSD slot; no changes are made to the B&N software. I discuss this in detail in Chapter 7, the famed Part of Tens.

Making a WishList

You can't always get what you want…but you can make lists about it. In fact, you can make multiple lists of wishes: one on your NOOK HD or HD+ and one on www.BN.com. The most important difference between the two is that the NOOK WishList is only for downloadable files. The website list can include paper books and other items you want to have shipped to you, as well as e-books, magazines, and newspapers that can be downloaded to the NOOK device. See Figure 5-13.

Figure 5-13: Dream on: a WishList of books, magazines, and other items; the version stored on the NOOK has only downloadable material.

Adding to your WishList

To add an item to your WishList that's held within the covers of your NOOK HD or HD+, do this:

1. **Go to the NOOK Shop.**

2. **Tap the cover or icon for a book, magazine, video, app, or other downloadable item to see its details.**

3. **Tap the WishList icon (a small heart with a +).**

   You'll get a message that the item has been added to your WishList. If you change your mind, tap the heart again to take it off.

Checking your WishList

To view your WishList on the NOOK, do this:

1. **Go to the Home screen of the NOOK Shop or any of the shop's category pages.**

2. **Tap the Wishlist icon (a small heart).**

   The icon will be in the system bar at the bottom of the page.

3. **Drool over your WishList, or pull the trigger and buy something: Tap an item and then confirm your intentions.**

Starting a Wishlist on the B&N website

You can create a similar WishList on the Barnes & Noble website:

1. **On a personal computer or your NOOK, go to** www.BN.com **or** www.nook.com.

2. **Tap the WishList icon (heart) for any item you want to keep track of.**

   On the website version, you can include printed books and other physical items that would have to be shipped to your home.

To see your WishList from the website, do this:

1. **Tap or click the My Account button.**

2. **Tap or click the My WishList button.**

   You'll see each item's cover, title, and price, along with the date you added it to your list.

To buy something on your online WishList, do this:

1. **Tap the price button next to the item.**

2. **Tap the Confirm button.**

Archiving to the NOOK Cloud

Have you ever been accused of walking around with your head in a cloud? So have I. And so, too, does your NOOK HD or HD+. Every registered user is automatically set up with unlimited storage in what Barnes & Noble calls the NOOK Cloud. So what's a *cloud?* Think of it as off-site storage that you can get to over the Internet.

Every title you buy from the NOOK Shop comes from a computer system somewhere in the B&N universe. A copy is downloaded to your NOOK for you to read or use locally. But at the same time, a record is kept of the purchase you've made.

Here's how that record comes in handy:

- ✔ **Sync:** You can *sync* your reading material across as many as six different NOOK devices or NOOK reading apps on personal computers, tablets, or smartphones. If you start a book on your NOOK HD+, you can continue on your smartphone as you commute to work, and finish it on the PC or Mac at your desk when the boss isn't looking.

- ✔ **Archive:** If you want to clear some space in the built-in or microSD card storage of your device, you can *archive* items from your NOOK to the NOOK Cloud. The file is removed from your NOOK, leaving behind only an icon or picture of its cover to remind you; any time you want to get that reading material, you can un-archive it from the NOOK Cloud.

- ✔ **Restore:** If your NOOK HD or HD+ should ever be stolen or damaged or permanently deceased, you can restore all files from the NOOK Cloud to a new device or app.

You can get the following items from the NOOK Cloud:

- ✔ Books
- ✔ Magazines
- ✔ Newspapers
- ✔ Catalogs
- ✔ Apps (reinstallation only)
- ✔ Videos (reinstallation only)

Not included: your personal files that you side loaded from a computer or downloaded over the Internet. (Chapter 4 explains side loading.) However, you can connect your NOOK to a computer and make a backup folder of your personal material there.

Moving an item to the NOOK Cloud

To use the NOOK Cloud, you need to have an active connection to the Internet through the Wi-Fi system.

1. **Press and hold on an item's cover.**

   A pop-up menu opens.

2. **Tap Move to NOOK Cloud.**

   The item is removed from your NOOK and a copy saved in the NOOK Cloud. See Figure 5-14.

Figure 5-14: Tap Move to NOOK Cloud to archive a book, magazine, newspaper, or catalog; you can easily retrieve it later.

Getting back an item from the NOOK Cloud

Make sure your NOOK is connected to the Internet through the Wi-Fi system, and then proceed:

1. **Find the item's cover or icon in your Library.**

   It'll be marked with a download arrow.

2. **Tap the cover or icon.**

   Allow the system to put the file back on your tablet.

Looking at your NOOK Cloud storage

Connect to the Internet, and then do this:

1. **Go to the Library on your NOOK HD or HD+.**

2. **In the system bar, tap the Contents icon (four stacked dotted bars).**

   A menu opens.

3. **Tap View Archive. See Figure 5-15.**

Figure 5-15: You can see what you've archived on the NOOK Cloud by pressing the Contents menu in the Library.

Be sure you understand the difference between *archiving* and *deleting.* If you *archive* an eligible item, you can get it back from the NOOK Cloud. If you *delete* any item, you erase it from your NOOK and can't get it without going back to the original source.

After you buy a book from Barnes & Noble, you own the license to that title on any device or application (up to the limit of six) registered to your account. You can leave the book file on your NOOK HD or HD+, or you can archive it back to your account, which removes it from the tablet but keeps it in your available material in the NOOK Cloud maintained by B&N. The key is that all devices or applications must be registered to the same account; as many as six devices are allowed.

Performing a sync or refresh

You can also refresh, or *sync,* your NOOK HD or HD+ to your BN.com account; doing so keeps it updated with all your currently purchased content — except for those you archived. Syncing lets you know about tablet updates, book loan offers, and other notices.

Follow these steps:

1. **Make sure your NOOK HD or HD+ Wi-Fi system is enabled and the device is successfully connected to the Internet.**

2. **Press the ∩ button to go to the Home screen.**

3. **Tap Library in the nav buttons.**

4. **Tap the menu icon (a stack of four dotted bars) in the lower left.**

   A menu opens. You can see the command in Figure 5-14 earlier in this chapter.

5. **Tap Refresh to start syncing your Library files.**

Taking your NOOK on a tour of a B&N Store

What happens if you take your NOOK HD or HD+ to an actual Barnes & Noble store (where there are walls and floors and ceilings)?

✔ The device asks if you'd like to connect to the InStore network. (Tap the Connect button to agree; tap the Dismiss button disagree.)

✔ If you do connect to the Wi-Fi network at the store, you can get:

✔ A free pass to read or sample most NOOK e-books for one hour per day free. You can read as many books as you want while you're in the store, although the 60-minute limit applies for each title.

✔ Exclusive content and offers available only to NOOK owners using the in-store network.

Lending and Borrowing Books

The primary key to the LendMe program is the NOOK Friends network — people who are in your circle. You've invited them or they've invited you. Once they accept an invitation, you can lend and borrow books with the press of a few buttons. See Figure 5-16.

You also can lend a book to someone who isn't a NOOK Friend. I explain that process later in this section.

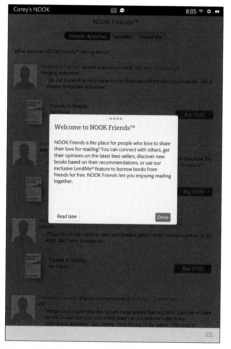

Figure 5-16: You can add NOOK Friends from different sources on your tablet.

You can invite friends from your Contacts list, from Facebook or Google, or by email:

1. **Make sure your NOOK device's Wi-Fi system is enabled and the device is successfully connected to the Internet.**

2. **Press the ∩ button to go to the Home screen and display the nav buttons.**

3. **Tap the Apps button.**

4. **Tap NOOK Friends.**

5. **Tap the Add Friend icon (person with a +).**

6. **Choose a source of friends:**

   • **Find Friends from My Contacts**

   • **Find Friends from Facebook**

   • **Invite a Friend via Email**

Lending a book to NOOK Friends

Books that you can loan sport a LendMe badge on their cover. To lend a book from your Library, open the LendMe app. You can open the LendMe app several ways:

Method one:

1. **Press the ∩ button to go to the Home screen.**

2. **Tap Apps.**

3. **Tap the NOOK Friends app.**

4. **Tap the LendMe tab at the top of the screen if it isn't already selected.**

5. **Scroll and then tap the LendMe button next to the book you want to loan.**

Method two works when the book appears on the Active Shelf or on the desktop part of the Home screen, or in your Library:

1. **Press and hold the book's cover.**

   A pop-up menu opens.

2. **Tap LendMe.**

Method three:

1. **On the Active Shelf, or the Home screen desktop, or in the Library, double-tap a book's cover.**

You'll see its details page.

2. If you can loan the book, tap the LendMe button.

Method four works when you're in the e-book itself:

1. Tap the center of the page to display the reading tools.

2. Tap the Discover icon.

A window will open, allowing you to rate the book, write a review, recommend the title, or lend it.

3. Tap the Share button.

After performing any one of these sets of commands, you will be greeted with a dialog box appears. From there, tap the icon that indicates how you want to notify someone of the LendMe offer:

✔ Send an email by selecting one of your Contacts. If you haven't entered any contacts or linked your account, select Contacts and press the Add Contact button.

✔ Post an offer on the person's Facebook wall. You must have previously linked your NOOK Tablet to your Facebook account.

✔ Send an automatically generated notification by Google Gmail if you've linked your NOOK Tablet to that account.

Lending a book of NOOK Friends

You can loan an e-book to a friend who isn't a NOOK Friend. All you need is a means of communication: email address or a Facebook connection. See Figure 5-17.

Figure 5-17: You can send a LendMe offer from your contacts, Facebook, or by an invitation via email.

Here's how:

1. **Confirm the lines of communication.**

    - **To make a LendMe offer by email:** Make sure you've entered your friend's email address into the Contact app on your NOOK. (Get to Contacts by tapping the Apps button on the Home screen.)

    - **To make a LendMe offer through Facebook:** Make sure you've linked your NOOK to your Facebook account. Make sure that the friend to whom you want to loan the book is in your Friends list on Facebook.

2. **Go to the Library on your NOOK.**

3. **Press and hold the cover of a book you want to lend.**

    Only books with a LendMe badge are eligible.

4. **In the menu that opens, tap LendMe.**

    A dialog box explains the terms of the loan. It also asks if you want to communicate with your friends through your Contacts list or through Facebook.

5. **Tap Contacts or Facebook.**

    The steps diverge from then on. Follow according to your choice.

If you tap Contacts: A window lists your contacts.

6. **Tap the name of the friend to whom you want to loan the book.**

7. **Tap in the Message field, and use the keyboard to write a message to your friend.**

8. **Tap the Send button to email the LendMe offer and message.**

If you tap Facebook: A window lets you post a LendMe offer on a friend's Facebook wall.

6. **Tap the Select a Friend button.**

7. **Tap the name of the person to receive the offer.**

8. **Tap in the Message field and use the keyboard to type a message.**

9. Tap the Post button to post the LendMe offer and message on your friend's Facebook wall.

Here are the conditions for the LendMe program from Barnes & Noble:

- ✓ While your book is loaned out, you can't read it on your own device.

- ✓ Not all books can be loaned; some publishers don't allow that. Look for a LendMe badge on a book cover.

- ✓ You can loan a book just once, and for no more than 14 days. A user can return the book any time during the loan. If it hasn't been returned at the end of 14 days, it's automatically returned.

- ✓ You can only lend from a registered NOOK device to users of other registered B&N devices, or applications that run on other devices such as desktop or laptop computers, smartphones, and certain other tablets.

- ✓ You can lend a book from anywhere with supported wireless connectivity (including Wi-Fi hotspots outside of the U.S., U.S. territories, and Canada).

- ✓ You can send LendMe offers to any email address, but to accept, the recipient must have an email address associated with a Barnes & Noble online account, and that means a resident of the United States or Canada. An offer expires after seven days if it hasn't been accepted.

- ✓ You can't loan a book that has been loaned to you.

- ✓ You can't save a borrowed book to the microSD card or archive it to the NOOK Cloud.

Another way to loan a book without restriction is to lend the actual NOOK HD or HD+ device to a trusted friend or acquaintance. If you do this, be aware that the person will have access to the Barnes & Noble store under your account name (but can't buy anything if your account requires a password to do so).

Borrowing a book

You can also reach out and ask someone to lend you a book from their Library. To find out who has lendable books, launch the LendMe application.

Here's how:

1. **Make sure your NOOK tablet's Wi-Fi system is enabled and the device is successfully connected to the Internet.**

2. **Press the ∩ button to display the Home screen and the nav buttons.**

3. **Tap the Apps button.**

4. **Tap NOOK Friends.**

5. **If the LendMe tab at the top of the screen isn't already selected, tap it.**

   You'll see these shelves:

   • **My Lendable Books.** Books of yours that you can loan.

   • **Friends' Books to Borrow.** All the libraries combined of friends who have posted books for loan. You can scroll horizontally through the titles or type a name or title in the search bar at the bottom of the page.

   • **Offers from Friends.** Specific offers from friends who are suggesting you borrow one of their titles.

   • **Requests.** Messages from friends asking to borrow books from you.

6. **Tap the Borrow button next to the name of the book you want to read.**

Setting Library privacy

Do you really want all of your friends to know the titles of all the books you have available for borrowing? Think it over: You may be disclosing some personal interests, political leanings, or other information you might want to keep to yourself. See Figure 5-18.

To decide what to keep to yourself, follow these steps:

1. **On the NOOK Friends page, tap the Privacy button.**

   The Privacy Settings page opens.

2. **Select (or deselect, if you want no books to show) the Show All of My Lendable Books to My NOOK Friends check box.**

Or: Add or remove a check mark next to the name of each of the lendable books in your Library.

Figure 5-18: If there are some books you don't want your friends to know you're reading, there's an app for that.

Managing Your Library

The Library is where all documents live on your NOOK, including books, periodicals, and personal files. The Library is all inclusive, while the individual panels for books, magazines, catalogs, and newspapers hold only files that the system recognizes as fitting that description.

To some extent, you actually can tell a book by its cover on the NOOK: not so much about what's inside, but a great deal about its status or stature in your collection.

- ✔ **New.** Freshly downloaded and ready to be opened. This badge goes away after the first time you open the document.

- ✔ **Sample.** A free sample of a book or other publication.

- ✔ **Download.** A publication that's either downloading or is waiting to be downloaded from www.BN.com.

- ✔ **Pre-order.** A title has been announced and is for sale, but isn't available for download yet. If you buy it, the book or publication will arrive at the first opportune moment.

- ✔ **Recommended.** A friend or contact has suggested that you check out this title.

✓ **LendMe.** A book that you can loan to someone.

✓ **Lent.** A book you are borrowing; the badge also indicates the number of days remaining on the loan. (While a book is loaned out, the original owner can't open it.)

Any search you start from your Library is done there only; if you start from the Home screen, the search expands, even looking at the NOOK Shop if it can't find the title you want already on your tablet.

Building your own shelves

You can build your own shelves. Separate them as you see fit to organize your collection. When your NOOK arrives, it includes just one shelf: Favorites. But how about adding shelves to hold your vast collection of *For Dummies* e-books, a few dozen of your favorite books by Corey Sandler, a special place for your cookbooks, and a separate group of emergency first aid guides in case something goes wrong in the kitchen but you are still able to read? See Figure 5-19.

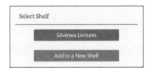

Figure 5-19: You can add custom shelves to hold particular groupings of publications or personal files.

Creating a shelf

You can create any shelf you want and call it anything you like. To create a shelf, do this:

1. **In My Library, tap the Contents icon** (a stack of four dotted bars.)

2. **Tap Create New Shelf.**

3. **Use the keyboard to enter a name for the shelf.**

4. **Tap Save.**

Adding items to a shelf

Now you need to move things to your shelf. To add items:

1. **Press and hold on a book or a file in the list of items in your Library.**

   A menu will appear.

2. **Tap Add to Shelf.**

3. **Tap the name of a previously created shelf, or tap Add a New Shelf.**

   You can rename a previously created shelf by tapping Rename a Shelf on the touchscreen. To remove a shelf, tap Remove a Shelf; tap OK to confirm.

In some rare cases you may need to unlock a book or periodical that you bought through Barnes & Noble and that's protected using Digital Rights Management (DRM). In that case just enter your name, the email address associated with the B&N account, and the credit card number that you used to make the purchase.

Going Elsewhere to Buy or Borrow

You can buy books from other sellers and download them to your NOOK. Many public libraries and educational institutions allow you to borrow reading material. Most of the files are in EPUB or PDF format, and they usually have Digital Rights Management (DRM) restrictions (to put a time limit on the loan of materials).

Lots of companies manage e-book loans with lots of tools. The leaders include Adobe Digital Editions and Overdrive. In addition, Amazon manages the lending process with its own Kindle tools. Other vendors of books, like Kobo, have their own systems.

About Adobe Digital Editions

The Adobe Digital Editions software is free and easy to use. See Figure 5-20.

Preparing to use a NOOK with Adobe Digital Editions

Follow these steps to get ready:

1. **On a desktop or laptop computer, use a web browser connected to the Internet and go to** www.adobe.com/ products/digitaleditions.

2. **Download the Adobe Digital Editions program to your PC or Mac.**

   Make sure it's the right version for your computer.

3. **Install the program on your desktop or laptop computer.**

4. **Follow the instructions to authorize your computer.**

5. **Turn on your NOOK HD or HD+.**

6. **Plug in both ends of the USB cable that came with your NOOK.**

   One end goes into the computer and the larger 30-pin connector goes into the NOOK Tablet. Make sure to use the right USB cord.

   Adobe "recognizes" the tablet.

Installing book files using Adobe Digital Editions

When you've put Adobe Digital Editions on your laptop or desktop computer, you can use it to buy or borrow books from stores or libraries that require it. Follow the store's or library's instructions to download files to your computer. Then do the following:

1. **Launch Adobe Digital Editions on your desktop or laptop computer.**

2. **Turn on your NOOK HD or HD+.**

3. **Plug in each end of the USB cable that came with your NOOK.**

   One end into the computer and the larger 30-pin connector goes into the NOOK Tablet. Make sure you don't force things!

4. **Drag files you have downloaded from their location on your computer's desktop or a folder onto the ADE library bookshelf.**

They will be available for reading on the computer, but your goal is to get them onto your NOOK.

5. **Follow the instructions to move those files to an authorized NOOK device.**

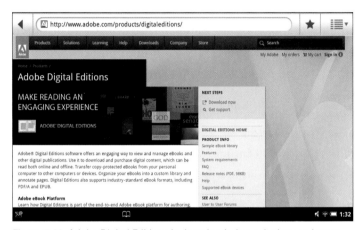

Figure 5-20: Adobe Digital Editions is downloaded to a desktop or laptop computer and used to authorize and then side load files to your NOOK.

Diving into Overdrive

Some stores and libraries use a program called Overdrive. In one version it works a lot like Adobe Digital Editions. A second version goes directly on tablet computers.

You can get a copy of Overdrive through the NOOK Shop for free; you'll also need a current library card from a participating institution. Some libraries are members of consortiums that expand the availability of both print and e-books. See Figure 5-21.

Using Overdrive is generally the same at all libraries, although there may be a few minor differences from place to place. Call or visit your library (bring them some cookies) if you need help.

1. **Download and install the Overdrive app on your NOOK Tablet.**

2. **Start Overdrive.**

3. **Log in to your local library using your library card number or password.**

4. **From within Overdrive, go to Get Books.**

   Browse through books by category or search for a specific title.

5. **Choose and download book files to your device.**

If you're borrowing from a library, the book may come with a time limit, usually 7 or 14 days. If you're buying from a store, the cost is charged to the account associated with the Overdrive app.

Figure 5-21: Many public libraries use Overdrive to loan e-books; here a group of libraries in my area are joined in an association cutely called CLAMS (Cape Libraries Automated Materials Sharing.)

Using Google Play Bookstore

You can buy a book at the Google e-bookstore within Google Play and start reading it on a NOOK, Maybe you want to continue reading the same book on your iPhone as you commute to work, read some more on the computer at your desk (during lunch hour, of course), and go out to dinner with a Sony e-reader. As with the NOOK store, the books are tied to your account — not to a specific piece or brand. See Figure 5-22.

Figure 5-22: The Google e-bookstore can provide current and classic literature.

Reading a public domain book via Google e-bookstore

To read a public domain book, follow these steps:

1. **Go to** `http://books.google.com/ebooks.`

2. **Choose the book.**

3. **Save it to your personal computer.**

4. **Connect your NOOK to the computer using the USB cable.**

   Careful there. Make sure to use the cable came with your NOOK and make sure the right end goes into the right device.

5. **Load the file from the computer to the tablet.**

   Read how to side load in Chapter 3.

6. **Install the latest version of Adobe Digital Editions on your laptop or personal computer.**

   If you haven't already, I explain how to do that earlier in this chapter.

7. Enter an Adobe ID if prompted.

If you don't have an Adobe ID, you'll see a link on-screen to get one. From that point, anytime you buy an item online with a service (like Google e-bookstore) that requires Adobe Digital Editions, the item is automatically associated with your Adobe ID, rather than your computer.

Buying on Google e-bookstore

And now, here's how to buy a book on Google and move it to your NOOK:

1. Go to `http://books.google.com/ebooks.`

2. Open a free account with Google.

The same account tags along if you use other Google tools, including Gmail.

3. Select a book.

4. Click Buy.

5. Pay for the license to own a copy of the book.

The file is added to your Google account.

6. In the list, find the book you want to transfer to the NOOK.

7. Click the About This Book button.

8. Click Read On Your Device.

You may see an EPUB version, a PDF version, or both.

9. Click one of the links to transfer the ACSM file onto your computer.

Be sure you know where the file is stored. You need the file to unlock the book. If you're given a choice between an EPUB or a PDF file format for an e-book, go with EPUB: It is more likely to include most or all current features for the NOOK include reflowable type, adjustments to typefaces, and more.

10. Find the ACSM file on your computer.

It may be in a Downloads folder or on the desktop. If you can't find the file, search for ***.acsm**.

11. Click the ACSM file.

The document should open in Adobe Digital Editions. If clicking the file doesn't open the Adobe software, find ADE on your computer (in My Programs) and start the program. Then select Add Item to Library from the Library menu, and find the ACSM file on your computer.

12. **If you aren't in Library view, click the icon in the top-left corner.**

    The book you bought from Google e-bookstore doesn't show up in the All Items bookshelf in the Library view.

13. **Turn on your NOOK HD or HD+.**

14. **Connect your NOOK to the computer with the provided USB cable.**

    Adobe Digital Editions should recognize your NOOK Tablet as an authorized device and display it on the left pane of the software. If you don't see your NOOK device listed, close Adobe Digital Editions and then reopen it with the USB cable in place, connected to your powered-on NOOK HD or HD+.

15. **Click and drag the Google e-book in the right pane onto the NOOK icon in the left pane.**

    If you can't drag a book from the library to the NOOK, the Adobe software hasn't recognized your tablet as an authorized device. Consult the Adobe help screens.

    If you want to confirm the transfer, click the NOOK icon and find the book file there.

16. **Eject the NOOK device from your laptop or personal computer before unplugging it.**

    Windows users can go to Explorer to find the NOOK and its memory card; right-click each and choose Eject. Macintosh users will find similar icons for the tablet in the Finder.

Getting something for nothing

Visit these worthy sites for great free reads from authors who no longer need the money:

✔ **Project Gutenberg at** www.Gutenberg.org. Some of the files are plain text that you have to format and change to use. See Figure 5-23.

✔ **Manybooks.net at** www.Manybooks.net. Some of the same books you'll find on Project Gutenberg along with some new work by current authors.

✔ **Feedbooks at** www.Feedbooks.com. Plenty of 19th-century classics for free, plus a store of books for sale.

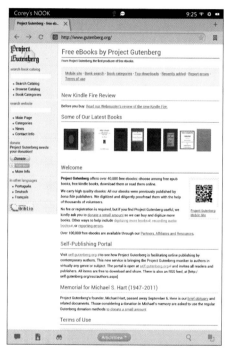

Figure 5-23: Project Gutenberg aims to digitize older, out-of-copyright books and publications.

Loading the right Calibre

Calibre is a free program you can download and install on your personal computer (Windows, Macintosh, or Linux). It converts files into EPUB or PDF format. With it you can also convert a PDF to a more flexible EPUB file. Get a copy of Calibre at http://calibre-ebook.com.

Chapter 6

Going Wireless and Out on the Web

In This Chapter

▶ Using the web browser to go online

▶ Getting and sending emails

▶ Playing music, videos, and games

*A*t its heart, the NOOK HD or HD+ is a fancy device upon which you can read books, magazines, newspapers, and catalogs or watch video. It does all of that on its own, using a capable microcomputer.

But you have to feed it material. For that, the primary means is a wireless connection to the Internet. And if that connection is available, you might as well be able to use the NOOK as an Internet appliance: to browse the web, do a bit of shopping, and to send and receive email.

If you have a Wi-Fi system in your home or office, you should be able to connect to it and use your NOOK HD or HD+ and pay nothing extra for Internet access (beyond what you're already paying). NOOK owners can also use their device for free at a Barnes & Noble store. And when you travel away from home or store, you should be able to find a free Wi-Fi connection at places like public libraries or parks, or for a reasonable fee at pubs and cafes almost anywhere.

Working without a Wire

The NOOK HD or HD+ has two different wireless radio systems:

- ✔ Wi-Fi, which helps connect to a router and then to the Internet.
- ✔ Bluetooth, which is a short-range system that works with earbuds, external keyboards, and other, similar devices.

I start here with Wi-Fi. The Wireless Settings screen lets you turn Wi-Fi on or off and it lists all the wireless networks your NOOK HD or HD+ can find. The system asks if you want it to reconnect to any other network you have already used. The list of Wi-Fi networks includes the name assigned by its owner and how strong the signal is (a stack of curved lines). The more dark lines you see, the better the signal. See Figure 6-1.

- ✔ To connect to an open or unsecured network, tap the network's name.
- ✔ To connect to a *secured network* (one that requires a password), tap the network name and then tap in the Password box. Type the required password (sometimes called a *key*) and tap Connect.

Some free networks offered at retail establishments give you the login information when you buy a drink or other item (not truly free, then, eh?); some hotels offer free service to registered guests. And some people, including your humble author, have been known to wander the streets of a foreign city looking for an open Wi-Fi signal so that he can check the baseball scores and the political news. When you use this service, you may see all or none of the following:

- ✔ Terms and conditions
- ✔ A login screen
- ✔ Credit card information page (or other payment)

The NOOK will detect a locked network, but you'll have to open a web browser window to enter the required details.

Figure 6-1: The wireless settings screen is the gateway to Wi-Fi systems.

Using the web browser

The NOOK HD or HD+ isn't limited to reading e-books and the like; when it's connected to a Wi-Fi system, you're free to roam the Internet. The tablet's web browser is quite fast — assuming the wireless signal is strong and uninterrupted — and perfectly capable of playing video or music or showing static pages.

When the NOOK HD and HD+ were released in late 2012, Barnes & Noble said that its browser didn't yet support Adobe Flash Player, which is necessary for playing many types of video. However, in Chapter 7 (the world-renowned Part of Tens), I tell you how I stumbled onto a solution.

To access the web browser, follow these steps:

1. **Make sure your NOOK is connected to a Wi-Fi network.**

2. **Sign in if necessary.**

3. **Press the ∩ button to display the Home screen.**

4. **Tap Web from the nav buttons.**

The NOOK starts the web browser even if the Wi-Fi system is turned off; if you see a page that tells you the Internet is unreachable, go to the Wi-Fi settings and make sure the system is turned on and that a connection's available.

The NOOK web browser should be familiar to anyone who has used a browser to cruise the web on a personal computer. Because the operating system is based on Android, the browser has many of the features of Google's Chrome browser. Just as you can on a laptop, for example, you can open new windows to quickly move from one page to another. See Figure 6-2.

Figure 6-2: The standard NOOK browser should look quite familiar to any computer or tablet user.

Here are some of the features of the standard browser:

- ⊯ **Address bar.** Near the top of the page. To visit a different page, tap in the address bar. Use the keyboard to type in an address and then tap the Enter key.

- ⊯ **Back button.** To the left of the address bar, tapping the left arrow takes you to the page you most recently visited.

- ⊯ **Forward button.** If you've moved back a few pages, press the → to go forward.

- ⊯ **Bookmarks.** To the right of the address bar. Tap the tiny ribbon icon to open a window and bookmark favorite sites. (This is sometimes referred to as *Favorites* to distinguish from placeholders in a book.) You can view and edit the places you've visited *(browsing history)* and organize your favorites. Tap the thumbnail for the page you want to visit. See Figure 6-3. To bookmark a page, tap the star icon.

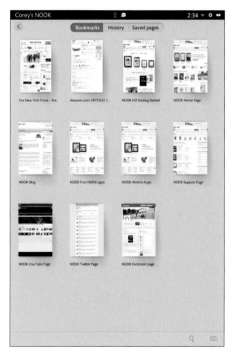

Figure 6-3: Bookmarks hold thumbnails so you can revisit favorite web pages. The History panel lets you return to places you've been recently.

✔ **New tab.** At the far right of the address bar, a + is what you tap when you want to open another tab in the browser without closing the original page.

✔ **Save pages.** Tap the icon of a page with a ↓ to save a thumbnail copy of the current page.

✔ **Article view.** One very, very nice feature of the standard NOOK HD or HD+ browser: You can reset whatever page you're currently looking at as a page of text. For example, Figure 6-4 shows the text-only version of the same web page shown earlier in this chapter.

Figure 6-4: The NOOK browser in Article view strips the bells and whistles on many web pages and lets you concentrate on the text.

Advanced browser functions

Even though the NOOK HD and HD+ are relatively small devices, their web browser packs many of the most valuable features. The portal to making changes is reached by tapping the favorites icon, the small ribbon at the right side of the address bar in the browser. See Figure 6-5.

Here's how to make some changes:

1. **Open the standard web browser.**

2. **Tap the favorites (star) icon at the right side of the address bar.**

3. **Tap any one of the tabs on the page: Bookmarks, History, or Saved Pages.**

4. **Press and hold on any of the thumbnails you see there.**

   A submenu opens.

5. **Tap your choice:**

   - **Open.** Open the page you can (barely) see in the thumbnail.

   - **Open in New Tab.** Open the page in a new tab in the browser, and keep the current page open.

   - **Edit Bookmark.** Open a page where you can use the keyboard to give a new name to a bookmark or change its address.

   - **Add Shortcut to Home.** This page is so important that you want to add a shortcut on the Home screen. Tapping that shortcut takes you directly to the web page without having to open the browser and find a favorite. Very slick, don't you agree?

   - **Share Link.** Send the link (the web address) to one of your contacts.

   - **Copy Link URL.** Have the NOOK keep the web address (URL) in memory; you can later paste that address in an email or note.

   - **Delete Bookmark.** This web page is no longer one of your favorites.

   - **Set as Homepage.** The browser will go here at the start of each session.

When you first use your NOOK web browser, the home page is set to be the Barnes & Noble store, which is devoted to all things NOOK. You're almost certainly going to want to return to the page at some time, but speaking for myself I don't need to be assaulted by advertising every time, all the time. I suggest making it a bookmark for easy access.

Figure 6-5: This menu lets you customize actions for the standard NOOK browser.

Adjusting the web browser's hair

The NOOK browser offers up five text sizes for web site text. Keep in mind that choosing a larger text size will make it easier to read but means you'll have to move around to see all the information on a page. See Figure 6-6.

To change the look of the text and background, follow these steps:

1. **With the browser open and running, tap the settings (gear) icon.**

2. **Tap Browser Settings at the top of the menu.**

3. **Tap Accessibility in the category list at the left.**

4. **Press and hold the white button in the Text Scaling slider, and move it left or right.**

   As you move the slider, you'll see the relative sizes of the cleverly named type sizes (tiny, small, normal, large, and huge) change.

   When you get it, your browser is set at 100 percent text scaling; many users will find that the optimum setting.

5. **Make other changes to your liking.**

The changes might include the amount of zoom that happens when you double-tap the screen, and the minimum font size that will appear.

6. **When you're finished, tap the ← to exit the menu.**

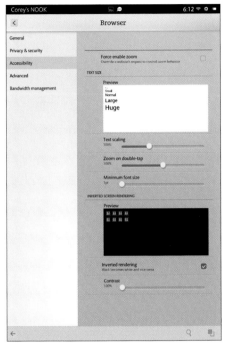

Figure 6-6: Browser accessibility settings let you change the web browser's text and the background.

To zoom in on a web page, quickly tap two times on the part you want to enlarge. Zoom out by tapping twice. After you zoom in, you can swipe left, right, up, or down to move around on the page. Using the zoom function makes more sense on some pages than enlarging the text type.

Configuring web privacy and security

There are people out there who know if you've been sleeping and know when you're awake. What's more, they know if you've been bad or good. For goodness' sake — or at least for your own confidentiality — pay attention to your web browser's privacy settings. See Figure 6-7.

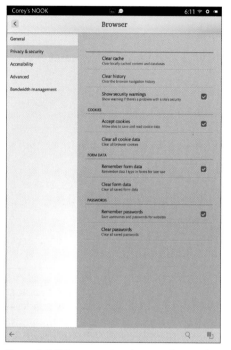

Figure 6-7: Privacy settings let you clear web pages, cookies, and history stored on a NOOK HD or HD+.

The NOOK HD or HD+ has only a basic set of security tools for Internet use. A clever Internet pirate may be able to get some of your personal information. Thieves are more attracted to laptop computers, but I recommend being picky about the information you store on your NOOK device, and about any information you type into the Internet.

✔ Your first line of defense: **Use tough passwords** on any accounts you visit (like www.BN.com), and change the passwords from time to time.

✔ Your second line of defense: **Pay attention to privacy settings** on the NOOK HD or HD+ and clear out personal information (like cookies) on a regular basis.

To get to *either* web privacy or security settings, follow along:

1. **Start the web browser.**

2. **Tap the settings (gear) icon in the right corner of the status bar.**

3. **Tap Browser Settings.**

4. **Tap Privacy & Security in the category listing on the left.**

5. **Choose amongst the options.**

Critical privacy and security options

Some of the most important privacy and security options are at the top of the page:

- ✓ **Clear Cache.** If you tell the NOOK to clear the cache (pronounced *cash*), it will erase information about sites you have visited.

- ✓ **Clear History.** To remove a list of recently visited web pages, tap here.

- ✓ **Show Security Warnings.** Tap to put a check mark in the box to be warned if there's a possible problem with a site's security certificate. That doesn't necessarily mean a threat to your privacy; it could just mean that a web page owner hasn't registered with all of the necessary watchdog agencies. If a warning pops up, use your judgment as to whether to proceed; when in doubt, avoid problematic pages.

Cookies

Alas, although your NOOK HD or HD+ is a technological marvel, it can't deliver your fresh chocolate chip cookies and milk after dinner. Some websites send a marker, a *cookie,* back to your tablet. The cookie indicates that you've visited, and sometimes shows choices or specific pages on the site you've explored.

Most cookies are benign. But some could tell unethical websites about your recent browsing behavior. And they also leave a trail behind that might reveal to others exactly where you've been browsing. I'm just saying . . .

Here are your options:

- ✔ **Accept Cookies.** This is turned on by default. To turn off this feature, clear the check mark. (Note that some websites may not respond properly if you turn off cookies.)
- ✔ **Clear All Cookie Data.** To delete cookies, tap the down arrow and then tap OK.

Form data

If you want to allow your NOOK device to fill in some of the blanks on various forms (including shopping carts), you can allow it to remember certain data. Or not.

- ✔ **Remember Form Data.** Your tablet can store data you've already typed into forms: things like your name, address, and phone number. This is turned on by default. To turn off this feature, clear the check mark.
- ✔ **Clear Form Data.** To clear any stored form data, tap the down arrow and then tap OK.

Web security options

If you're certain no one else will use your NOOK, you can allow it to remember certain passwords for you. Really? I would only let the NOOK do this if I also require a system password to be entered before the device can be used.

- ✔ **Remember Passwords.** If you tap to place a check mark in the box, the browser will ask you if you want to store usernames and passwords for websites. (Not all sites let you do this.)
- ✔ **Clear Passwords.** Tap to clear all saved usernames and passwords.

Advanced web page settings

The NOOK browser has some features that not even the most advanced and costly tablets offer — among them, full-screen pages rather than the small versions aimed at smartphones. See Figure 6-8.

Figure 6-8: Advanced settings include requests for full web pages instead of mobile versions, plus other controls over browsing function.

To get to them, do this:

1. **Start the web browser.**

2. **Tap the settings (gear) icon in the right corner of the status bar.**

   The Options menu is in the top right of the address bar; refer back to Figure 5-2. When you tap the Options arrow, a menu opens.

3. **Tap Browser Settings.**

4. **Tap Advanced in the category panel on the left side.**

Here are the most important options offered on this page:

✔ **Set Search Engine.** When you get your NOOK, it uses Google to search the web, which is appropriate considering that Google developed the browser used by the

NOOK. If you tap here, though, you can instead choose to use Yahoo or Bing.

✔ **Open in Background.** Tap a check mark into the check box to have new tabs open behind the current tab.

• **Enable JavaScript.** Many websites use JavaScript to show animation or special effects. You'll probably want to keep this on, although you might try shutting it off if you have problems with certain pages.

• **Enable Plug-Ins.** Most users will want to leave this at its default setting of Always On. If you suspect that a *plug-in* (an enhancement you may get from various sources) is causing problems, or if a technician tells you to make a change, you can tap here and instead choose On Demand or Off.

• **Default zoom.** Tap the ↓ to adjust how the tablet reacts to a double-tap for a zoom-in. Choices are Far, Medium, or Close. The default setting is Medium.

• **Auto-fit pages.** Leave the check mark to have the browser format pages to fit the screen.

• **Desktop Mode.** Leave the check mark to always request the full website instead of the sometimes less-capable mobile sites designed for tiny smartphone screens.

• **Block pop-ups.** The browser automatically blocks pop-ups (boxes that unexpectedly appear, and mostly to your annoyance). However, you may need or want to see them. You can block on or off from the Page Content settings of the web configuration options.

Sending and Getting Email

The NOOK HD or HD+ comes with email that lets you send and receive from most other email programs: an account you have set up on your own or a web-based email service like Gmail. See Figure 6-9. A few important notes:

✓ Your tablet must be connected to a Wi-Fi network to receive and send email.

✓ Barnes & Noble doesn't provide email accounts.

✓ You can see the 25 most recent messages for each account (that you've linked to the NOOK, anyway).

Figure 6-9: Give the username and password; then choose the right protocol. If you use a web-based service like Gmail, many details are taken care of.

Using the Email app

You may have already set up an email account when you initially set up your NOOK. In this section, I show you how to add a new email account. These steps assume you've already set up an email account with a provider (like Google for Gmail or with an Internet service provider like your telephone or cable television company).

To start and use the Email app, do this:

1. **Press the ∩ button to go to the Home screen.**

2. **Tap Email in the nav buttons.**

   You're taken to the Inbox. If you haven't visited the Email app yet, you're taken to a screen so you can set it up.

3. **With the Email app open, tap the settings (gear) icon.**

4. **Tap Email Settings.**

5. **Tap Add Account at the bottom of the Settings page.**

6. **Type the address for your email account.**

   It will be something like *myaddress@mydomain.com*.

7. **Enter the password for the account.**

8. **Optional: Tap the check box for Send Email from This Account by Default.**

   If you do so, the system always assumes that any outgoing mail will come from this account.

9. **Tap Next.**

   • If you're using one of the common web-based services (like Gmail, Hotmail, or Yahoo! Mail), this may be all you need to do. You're notified if all goes well.

   • If you're using your own domain or a less-popular mail service, you may have to proceed with a manual setup. I get to that in the next section.

10. **Optional: Type a name for this account.**

    A name can help you distinguish among multiple accounts. If you don't want to name the account, leave the option blank.

11. **Enter your name as you want it to appear in email messages that you send.**

    Recipients see this name in the From field on their Email app.

12. **Click Done.**

    Go forth and email.

Setting up an account manually

If automatic setup doesn't work, set up your Email app account manually. *You have to know the exact name of your provider's email server for sending and receiving.* You should be able to find that by consulting help or FAQ pages for the provider, by calling their help desk (some are more helpful than others), or by examining the Properties setting on an existing email program on your desktop or laptop computer.

To set up an email account manually, follow Steps 1-8 in the preceding section. Then do this:

9. **Tap Manual Setup.**

   The Server Settings screen opens.

10. **Tap an account type: POP or IMAP.**

    A POP account stores all mail on your computer or tablet; an IMAP account keeps the mail on a central server and sends copies to your tablet or PC. Each has advantages; I use IMAP because I travel a lot and prefer the security of knowing that my email is being backed up and stored remotely.

    If all of this POP, IMAP, and port number stuff makes your head spin, stop and take a deep breath. Then use the telephone to call customer service at your Internet provider or consult their online FAQ pages. Trust me, this is a question they get a few thousand times per day and they'll know exactly what information you need. Write down the necessary information and keep it in a secure place, but *don't* include your password on the same note.

11. **Tap OK.**

12. **Enter the name of the POP or IMAP server for incoming mail.**

    For example, it might be something like IMAP.*isp_ server.com.*

    Some systems have extra security requirements or use a non-standard port (the gateway from your tablet to the Internet). Unless your provider has told you otherwise, leave these settings unchanged.

13. **Tap Next.**

   If the NOOK finds your email provider, it shows you
   another setup screen.

14. **Enter the name of the SMTP server for outgoing
    email, if you're prompted for it.**

   An example might be something like SMTP.*isp_server.
   com*. See Figure 6-10.

   If all goes well, you see one final page with options
   about how often the system checks for new mail.

15. **Tap Done. You're done.**

Figure 6-10: If you use your own mail domain or a less-common service,
get your server name and other specific information from your
email provider.

Sending an email

Sending a message is very simple. If you've set up more than one email account, you can choose which one to use for the outgoing message by tapping the ↓ beside Mailbox at the top of the Email screen.

1. **Tap the envelope icon in the lower left. See Figure 6-11.**

2. **Use the keyboard to type an address in the To box.**

   If you want to send the message to more people, you can separate their addresses with commas. Or, you can tap the ↓ beside the CC/BCC button at the upper right and enter addresses for a copy or a blind copy.

Tap to start a new email.

Figure 6-11: You can send an email from any storage place of the app; in this case I'm rooting through the trash. The icon to send a new message is in the lower left.

If you enter an address in the BCC (blind copy) field, people who got the original message or the CC copy won't see the names of those recipients.

3. **Enter a subject.**

Actually, you don't *have to,* but it is considered good Internet protocol to do so. In fact, I usually ignore messages that don't have a subject because many of that sort are spam and I hate spam.

You can use the Tab key on the keyboard to move from one field to another. For example, when you're done typing a name or address in the To box, tap the Tab key to jump to the Subject box.

4. **Type a message.**

You can attach a photo or other type of file by tapping on the paperclip icon and selecting a location where the file can be found. See more details later in this chapter.

5. **Tap Send.**

Your NOOKy Hancock

When you send a message from your NOOK HD or HD+ Email app, this is tagged on at the bottom of every one: "Sent from my NOOK." If you'd rather not send advertising, change your signature:

1. Tap the settings (gear) icon in the status bar (on the Home screen).

2. Tap All Settings.

3. Tap Applications in the Category panel on the left.

4. Tap Email in the Settings list on the right.

5. Tap one of your accounts in the Email Settings panel on the left.

6. Tap Signature in the Settings panel on the right.

7. Edit or delete the text you find in the Signature block.

8. Tap OK.

Replying to or forwarding a message

Forwarding a message sends a copy of the message to someone else. The process is nearly identical to that of Reply. Here's how:

1. Open an email message.

2. Tap Reply.

Some day you're going to thank me for this one: Be *very careful* before you choose Reply All if you intend to crack wise, complain, or pass along some comment you may someday regret. Choose Reply All only after you have duly considered all of the potential consequences and studied all of the addresses to which your response will be sent.

3. Tap Forward.

The Compose screen opens.

4. Type the email addresses to send the message to.

You can add a note of your own, like "This is the funniest joke I've ever heard." (That was the reason the Internet was invented, I believe.) The original subject line goes along with the message, along with Fwd:. You can edit the subject if you'd prefer.

5. Tap Send.

Look carefully at a message before you send it. Do you really want *all* recipients to know *all* of the information it has? Are you possibly violating someone's expectation of privacy by passing along *all* email addresses? Remember, too, that a recipient of a forwarded message might choose to forward it to a new group of people, spreading its contents (and email addresses) to people you don't know. I generally edit out all unnecessary information from messages I forward.

Deleting email

To get rid of a message you have open, tap the trash can at the bottom of the screen.

If the message you want to get rid of isn't open, go to the Inbox or any other of the boxes (Drafts, Outbox, Sent, Trash, and more) and follow these steps:

1. **Tap the check box next to the message(s) you want to delete.**

2. **Tap the trash can icon at the lower-left corner of the screen.**

Getting attached

Can you remember your first attachment? The thrill of victory, the agony of defeat.

Enough about high school. Let's talk about our mature, modern lives. A time when we use our high-tech computer tablets to send photographs of the grandchildren, video clips of cats stuck in shoe boxes, and singing birthday cards. Most of those are sent as *attachments* to emails, which means you're sending a separate file along with the text of a message.

If you get a message with attachments, tap the View Attachments button.

 The NOOK HD or HD+ can display PDF files or Microsoft Office word processing, spreadsheet, and simple PowerPoint files. The NOOK will store email attachments in the MyFiles/ Downloads folder.

Feeling Bluetooth?

 The second radio system in the NOOK HD and HD+ is called *Bluetooth.* That's an odd name, at least for those of us who aren't of Scandinavian heritage. The word comes from a nickname for tenth-century king Harald I of Denmark, who united a bunch of Danish tribes into a single kingdom. Somehow that became the name of a communication protocol that united all sorts of technologies.

Here's what Bluetooth does: It lets your NOOK quickly and easily connect to another device separated by a fairly short distance. On the NOOK HD and HD+, Bluetooth is used to connect earbuds and headsets to listen to audio. We can also hope to see devices like external keyboards and perhaps other peripherals.

Follow along:

1. **Press the ∩ button to go to the Home screen.**

2. **Tap the settings (gear) icon.**

3. **Tap All Settings.**

4. **Tap the Wireless & Bluetooth settings page.**

5. **Tap the On button for Bluetooth.**

Connecting devices using Bluetooth is pretty simple. One device — the NOOK HD or HD+ in this case — is told to *listen* for a connection request. The other device is told to broadcast its willingness to electronically mate. In Figure 6-12 you can see the results of a pairing between my NOOK HD+ and a Jabra earbud; the music was spectacular.

Figure 6-12: The tiny speakers in the NOOK HD or HD+ are adequate at best; use an earbud or other audio system connected by Bluetooth to improve the quality.

App-lying Yourself

Your NOOK HD or HD+ runs a customized version of the Android operating system. That's a very good thing, because Android (developed by Google) has been adopted by a wide range of smartphones and tablets; because of that, lots of people have made *applications* (or *apps* — small programs) that can run on these devices. See Figure 6-13.

Figure 6-13: All your apps are on a shelf that you can get to from the Library. You can also put shortcuts to apps on the Home screen.

At least officially, the only source of add-on programs for the NOOK HD or HD+ is through the NOOK App Store.

The supplied apps

The NOOK Tablet comes with some applications. Press the ∩ button to display the nav buttons and then tap Apps. The first release of the NOOK HD and HD+ didn't have games like chess and Sudoku (which had been thrown in with earlier NOOK models). Here are the apps that came with the first release of the tablet:

✏ **Contacts.** A manager for names, addresses, phone numbers, and email addresses. Once you add a contact, you can use it in the Email app as well as the social network apps.

✔ **Music Player.** With this program you can play music files that you've downloaded (or side loaded; see Chapter 3) to your NOOK. I discuss the player in the next section of this chapter.

✔ **Gallery.** This all-purpose picture collector and video player works with files you downloaded or side loaded to your NOOK. (Again, see Chapter 4 for side loading instructions.)

✔ **NOOK Friends.** This is Barnes & Noble's own version of a social network combined with a lending library. You can communicate with those you have befriended, sharing recommendations and comments and lending books — subject to certain restrictions.

✔ **Hulu Plus.** This service, for a monthly subscription price, has on-demand streaming video of television shows, movies, and other media. See Figure 6-14. It is jointly owned by the major television networks. The long-term prospects for this app are uncertain, since B&N plans to push its own NOOK Video service.

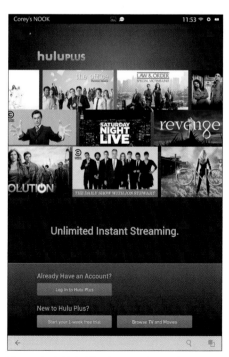

Figure 6-14: Hulu Plus has movies and tv shows as streaming files.

✔ **Pandora.** This free streaming audio service tailors its tunes to your preferences. You get to create and fine-tune your own stations. Play just one station, rotate through them all, or ask the computer to choose random songs you (will probably) dig.

Music player

Audio sounds a little better if you plug a set of earbuds into the headphone output jack. See Figure 6-15. The NOOK plays most of the common file formats, including MIDI, MPEG, WAV, AAC, and AMR.

Figure 6-15: The controls for the music player are simple and obvious.

Moving audio files onto the NOOK

To transfer audio files onto the NOOK HD or HD+:

1. **Connect your NOOK to a personal computer using the USB cable.**

Use the cable that came with the device or an identical cable; don't use a generic cable. (The cable detaches from the AC adapter; that end is a standard USB plug that you can attach to a desktop or laptop computer.)

On your desktop or laptop computer, the NOOK HD or HD+ shows up as a new disk drive called MyNOOK (or, on some devices, as a Removable Drive with a letter code or under its model name). If a microSD memory card is in your NOOK Tablet, it will also show up in My Computer (Windows) or in the Finder (Macintosh).

2. **Drag the files onto the NOOK drive or an attached microSD memory card.**

   Put audio files in the Music folder in My Files.

3. **Eject the media drive.**

The official instructions say ejecting a device is a must. Microsoft Windows usually has a Safely Remove Hardware icon in the system tray. Or go to My Computer, highlight and right-click the drive, and choose Eject. In my experience, it's not essential, but you're better safe than sorry.

4. **Unplug the USB cable.**

Playing an audio file from the Library

You can start the music player

- ✔ By tapping a music file
- ✔ By tapping the music player icon
- ✔ From the Library

Music Player modes

The music app has two modes: Browse and Now Playing. A red (not rock) band tells you which mode you're in. To switch modes, tap the icon in the upper-right corner of the screen. Tap three times on the ceiling if you're a Tony Orlando fan.

In Browse mode you can choose from these options:

- ✔ **Shuffle.** (Icon: two crossed arrows) The tablet randomly selects and plays songs from your collection.

✔ **Repeat.** (Icon: two arrows in a loop) Tap once to repeat all your songs; tap tap twice to repeat the current track.

✔ **Album art.** (Icon: a box) See artwork for the track that's playing.

✔ **Browse.** (Icon: a stack of horizontal lines) See available tracks.

✔ **Search.** (Icon: a magnifying glass) Hunt through your NOOK Tablet files to find a particular song or artist.

✔ **List.** (Icon: musical note) See songs and their playing times.

✔ **Artist.** (Icon: microphone) See songs by the artist's name.

When you're using the music player in Now Playing mode, you can press and hold the gray arrow (to the left of a song title) and drag the file up or down in the list to change the song order.

To use Hulu Plus you must have a membership; it's separate from your account with Barnes & Noble. If you have a previously established account, you can sign in to it from the NOOK; if not, you can set up one from the tablet or from a desktop or laptop computer.

Video Playing On

The NOOK HD and especially the HD+ has a high-resolution, full-color screen that's quite capable as miniature tv, although the screen size is obviously more suited for watching up close.

You can use this facility three ways:

✔ Visit websites that offer free video on demand. These include sites like www.youtube.com, computer and electronics review sites like www.cnet.com, and TV networks like www.nbc.com. For best results, choose a file intended for a tablet.

✔ Subscribe to services like Hulu Plus and Netflix.

✔ Watch videos that you've side loaded. (See Chapter 3 for instructions.) The videos may be ones you took with your video camera or cellphone, or they may be works you got elsewhere (following all copyright laws, please).

> Transfer compatible video files from a personal com-
> puter using the USB cable; follow the same instructions
> you would for transferring music and audio files. Those
> instructions are in this chapter's "Moving audio files onto
> the NOOK" section.

The best quality videos are in MP4 and M4V file formats. The
other acceptable file formats come from the small-screen
world of smartphones, including 3GP. To play a video that
you've loaded onto your NOOK device, find and tap it. (One
route: Tap the ∩ button; tap Library, and then tap My Stuff.
Find the file in the Video or Downloads folder.) If you try to
load and run a file that isn't supported, it simply won't play.

In most cases you can't enlarge a video that you're playing
from a file that's stored on the NOOK HD or HD+; the pinch-
out gesture may work with some streaming video websites,
though.

Subscribing to Hulu Plus

Hulu Plus brings current and older TV shows, and some
movies, to your tablet over the Internet on a monthly subscription basis. Shows generally have limited advertising.

Hulu Plus and Netflix videos are *streamed* to your device and
not stored on it. The only way to watch television shows or
movies offered by these services is with an active Wi-Fi connection to the Internet.

Your NOOK Tablet has an app that takes you directly to the
Hulu Plus website; you can also get there by using the web
browser and going to www.hulu.com/plus. You can sign up
for the service from your NOOK Tablet or from a desktop or
laptop computer. (The original free service, Hulu, isn't available on the NOOK Tablet.)

Subscribing to Netflix

Netflix is one of the main providers of streaming video
(and they're streaming to everything from PCs to Internet-
connected TVs, to handheld devices — including your NOOK
Tablet. You can sign up for a monthly subscription.

Netflix shows only in landscape mode on the tablet, and offers thousands of movies. Not all of the Netflix library is available to stream; some are offered only in DVD form. Visit www. netflix.com and explore some of the library.

Amazon Prime Video

Amazon Prime is another player in the video marketplace. Its streaming video is offered by the ubiquitous online retailer. You can get to it through the web browser on the NOOK HD or HD+ and play movies and tv shows from the collection on demand. See Figure 6-16. In Chapter 7, I explain a minor adjustment you may need to prepare your NOOK to use this service.

Amazon includes Prime as part of an annual package that offers faster shipping for purchases made from its online store.

Figure 6-16: Amazon Prime offers a collection of classic (like *Gallipoli*) and modern films and television shows.

NOOK Video: A work in progress

Barnes & Noble has large plans for its own service, NOOK Video. The company promises content from major studios and television producers, including HBO, Sony Pictures, STARZ, Viacom, Warner Brothers, and Walt Disney Studios.

Videos that you stream and download from the NOOK Shop are also backed up in the NOOK Cloud. That means you can watch what you've bought on different devices in addition to the NOOK HD and HD+. Just like you can with an e-book, you can start a movie on an Internet-connected tv, continue on a NOOK HD, and finish up on a personal computer with a NOOK Video app.

One key to moving the video from device to device is the developing UltraViolet technology, which adds a digital proof of purchase to files.

You and YouTube

YouTube is one of the hardest-to-fathom successes of the digital era. Like Wikipedia, it's almost impossible *not* to find a video about almost any subject: music, travel, politics, and a gazillion videos about cats playing in bags.

Search for a subject, troll through the listings, sit back, and enjoy. See Figure 6-17.

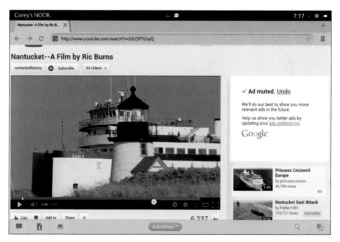

Figure 6-17: YouTube works like a tv with nearly infinite channels; here a scene from a documentary about Nantucket, the island where I live.

Chapter 7
Ten-Plus Tips and Tricks

In This Chapter

▶ Making screen captures

▶ Handling power troubles

▶ Enhancing your warranty

▶ Dealing with wireless problems

A printed book is not high tech. It has no batteries, no microprocessor, no screen. You can fix most technical failures of paper books with Scotch tape. But that's not true with high-tech device like the NOOK HD or HD+. Conditions change. Settings can go awry. Even pieces of hardware can become confused and stutter to a stop. In this chapter, I offer some advice on how to make things right.

But wait, there's more: In this section of the world-renowned Part of Tens that is included in nearly every For Dummies book, I show you a few hidden or secret tricks to expand the value of your NOOK. There's no need to count. When I talk about a part of tens, I don't stop after the ninth tip. That would be much too classically digital. (*Digital* as in a mathematical system based around units of ten, which made eminent sense tens of thousands of years ago when early humans finally realized that most of them were born with ten fingers and ten toes.)

Computer math is extensible and almost infinitely adjustable. There are binary systems (powers of two), decimal systems (tens), hexadecimal systems (a base of 16), and then there is this very special *NOOK HD For Dummies,* Portable Edition "No Extra Charge Additional Tips Section."

Making a Screen Capture

Here's a function you won't find in the official NOOK HD or NOOK HD+ user guide (at least in the first version of that publication). You can grab a *screen capture* (also called a *screenshot*) of almost anything displayed on your tablet.

Press the ∩ button and the - volume button — in that order — very closely together. You press the ∩ button about a tenth of a second before you press the – volume button. It may take more than a few tries to get the hang of it; if you've done it correctly, you'll see a picture of the screen appear in a box on the display for a moment and then zoom away.

The volume buttons are on the top side of the NOOK HD+, but on the right side of the NOOK HD.

If you tap the notifications icon at the top of the screen, you'll see confirmation that you've taken a screenshot. See Figure 7-1. The screenshot is automatically stored in a subfolder inside the Pictures folder of your NOOK HD or HD+.

You can see the screenshot:

✓ Tap the screenshot in the notifications menu.

✓ Press the ∩ button to go the Home screen. Tap Apps and then tap Gallery.

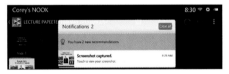

Figure 7-1: If you tap the notification icon, you'll see that a screenshot has been captured; tap the message to go directly to the Gallery to see it.

Because this feature is an "unofficial" one that is part of the underlying Android operating system, it is always possible that Barnes & Noble will improve, make worse, or delete the function. But as this book goes to press, users with quick and nimble fingers can grab images all day. I know I did.

Now suppose you want to use that screenshot to illustrate something. Like maybe nearly all of the illustrations in this book.

You have several ways to get the screenshot off your NOOK:

1. **Connect your NOOK to a PC or Mac using the supplied USB cable.**

2. **Once the connection is made, open the folder for the NOOK.**

3. **Go to My Files > Pictures > Screenshots.**

4. **Drag and drop the file(s) from the NOOK to a folder on your computer.**

Here's another way:

1. **On your NOOK, open the Email app.**

2. **Open a new message.**

3. **Enter an address; it can be your own.**

4. **Tap the paper clip icon.**

   A menu asks you to choose an attachment.

5. **Tap Gallery.**

6. **Tap the collection of screenshots and then tap the one you want to send.**

7. **Tap Send.**

Aaaaand one more way:

1. **Follow Steps 1-6 from the method just described.**

2. **With the Gallery displayed, open the Screenshots folder.**

3. **Press and hold on an image until a menu opens.**

4. **Tap Share.**

5. **Tap Email to send a message with the image attached. See Figure 7-2.**

Screenshots are saved as png files, which are *lossless* compressed files at the full screen resolution of 1280 x 1920 pixels on the NOOK HD+, or 900 x 1440 on the NOOK HD. In other words, the quality is very good and the size is quite reasonable.

Figure 7-2: You can see screenshots with the Gallery app. You can also send one by email by pressing and holding on its image.

When you make a screen capture, it's numbered this way: Screenshot_2012-11-12-10-37-58.png. That means this is a screenshot taken in 2012, on November 12, at 10:37 and 58 seconds. Can I suggest that you rename them something more meaningful? You can rename them when you store them on a computer, or you can use the computer to rename them on your NOOK when the two devices are connected with the USB cable.

And I say earlier, you can capture *almost* anything displayed on your NOOK. You can't grab a shot of the screen as you're setting up your NOOK device or when first starts up.

Reenergizing a Dead NOOK

Okay, not really a *dead* unit. But some things can make a NOOK seem dead (or seriously confused) even when it isn't ready for the recycle bin. The usual suspects include the following.

Not enough battery power

The NOOK tablet's rechargeable battery does not have an endless source of energy; you must recharge it. Depending on how you use your device (including whether you use the Wi-Fi system for an extended period of time), you may need to recharge the battery daily, or you may have to recharge it just once a week.

Your NOOK's lithium ion battery should deliver a nice charge for several years. If the battery fails during the standard one-year warranty period, you'll have to send it in for repair. Don't wait for one year and one day.

If your NOOK starts acting squirrely, check the battery level. Anytime the device is on the Home screen or in most text-based books, you will see a battery icon in the bottom-right corner.

To see details of battery use and performance, do this:

1. **Tap the Settings gear icon.**

2. **Tap All Settings.**

3. **Tap Device Information (in the category panel on the left).**

4. **Tap Battery (on the right). See Chapter 2.**

Modern high-capacity rechargeable batteries get warm as they're used. It's highly unlikely, but a faulty battery could be a fire risk. If you think the internal battery is generating too much heat or is otherwise acting odd, turn the thing off and contact Barnes & Noble customer service at 1-800-843-2665.

Now, consider things you can do to make the battery last as long as possible:

✔ **Don't let the battery run down completely.** Turn off the tablet when you see the low charge alert. Recharge the battery fully before you use it again.

✔ **Avoid extremely high or low temperatures.** Don't take your tablet with you on the ski chairlift or into the sauna.

✔ **Don't let your battery get scorching hot while the tablet's running.** If your tablet is so hot you could fry an egg on it as you read the morning newspaper, do these three things:

- Carefully unplug it.
- Turn off the power.
- Call B&N customer service at 1-800-843-2665.

✒ **Recharge the battery before a prolonged period on the shelf.** If you plan to put your tablet away for more than a week, charge the battery until it's at least half full. Then turn it off completely by pressing and holding the power button for 3 seconds.

Your recharger isn't getting juice

I'm pretty advanced when it comes to technical matters, but I do have a confession to make: I once paid a washing machine repairman to come over and tell me that the reason the machine wasn't performing properly was because the water faucet was turned off. The same sort of situation can arise with a battery recharger. Make sure it's plugged into a live outlet; try to avoid using an outlet that is controlled by a wall switch. If the charger is attached to a power strip, make sure that device is on. You can test an outlet or strip by plugging a lamp into it.

The recharger design can also be mischievous. There is a charger, and a separate USB cable runs between the charger and the tablet. Make sure that the cable is properly and fully attached at each end and that the little LED on the tablet beside the cable glows. It's orange while it charges and green when it's done charging.

Barnes & Noble urges you to use only the AC adapter and the USB cable that came with your NOOK HD or HD+. If you need a second charger, they'll be happy to sell you one. (That's not to say that other manufacturers may not offer their own fully capable version of the charger. If you choose to use a charger from another company, make certain it exactly matches the electrical specifications of the manufacturer's original device.)

You can also buy a car charger for your NOOK HD or HD+; check the www.nook.com accessories page or your local Barnes & Noble store. Please, though: Don't read a book while driving down I-95. I might just use my smartphone to call the cops.

Keeping a NOOK Tablet Happy

The NOOK is an electrical device. To keep it happy, keep it cool, dry, and all together in one piece.

- ✔ **Keep it dry.** Don't take the NOOK into the bathtub with you — or out into a thunderstorm or into the steam room. I also strongly suggest keeping cups and cans of caffeine far away. A little bit of water can wreck the tablet.

- ✔ **Keep it cool.** Never leave the NOOK in a closed car in the summer heat, and don't put it on a radiator in the winter.

- ✔ **Keep it in one piece.** Although the NOOK is reasonably sturdy, don't put it in your back pocket or use it to prop a rocking table.

Piloting Your NOOK at 33,000 Feet

You're likely to be asked to turn off your NOOK in places like airplanes, hospitals, and laboratories. Follow the instructions of flight attendants, doctors, nurses, and anyone else who has a real reason to ask.

However, what they're (usually) really asking is that you turn off the Wi-Fi and Bluetooth radios. There's an app for that:

1. **Tap the Settings gear icon in the status bar.**

   The status bars appears at the top of most screens. If you need to, press the ∩ button to go to the Home screen.

2. **Tap the slide switch beside Airplane Mode to On.**

   Your Wi-Fi and Bluetooth radios are turned off, but otherwise, you can read and use other utilities that don't require the Internet. When it's safe to use the radios, return to this panel and turn off Airplane Mode.

The biggest concern is the Wi-Fi radio, although (just between you and me) I think this is a bogus issue. Wi-Fi is just about everywhere now, including hospitals and airplanes. A slightly bigger concern would be cellular systems, although even that is probably not a real issue except on board an airplane; it's not a matter of interference with the plane's electronic systems, but the fact that a cellphone trying to connect with cell towers on the ground could easily end up linking to dozens of antennas at the same time.

Rubbing Your Prints off the Touchscreen

You should keep your touchscreen clean for three good reasons:

- It might stop responding to your touch if there is too much gloop on it.
- The image will look pretty bad if you have to view it through a layer of french fry grease.
- Do you really want people to see your handsome, high-tech NOOK HD or HD+ covered with smudges, smears, and schmutz?

Try to keep your hands clean; don't go out and change the oil in your car and then swipe your fingers across the touchscreen. Clean up first. Also, consider buying a little home for your NOOK. A carrying case or sleeve can help protect and keep it clean.

Here's how to clean the touchscreen:

1. **Press and hold the power button for about 3 seconds to turn off the NOOK.**

2. **Wipe with a soft cloth.**

    I recommend using one of those specialized microfiber cloths made for cleaning eyeglasses.

- *Don't* use any chemicals to clean the screen. If necessary, you can make the cloth *slightly* damp.
- *Don't* run the screen (or the cloth) under the faucet.

Improving Your NOOK Warranty

Your NOOK comes with a warranty. Don't be shy about calling technical support or visiting a Barnes & Noble store and seeing their specialist for help.

The basic warranty from Barnes & Noble protects against unit failure. If the screen stops lighting up, the speakers buzz instead of sing, or if Wi-Fi is no longer wide nor of good fidelity, the company promises to repair or replace it with an equivalent model (which may be new or may be a "remanufactured" model returned by a previous owner). This sort of warranty is standard.

It's important to understand what the warranty doesn't cover:

- A tumble to the floor.
- Getting caught in a folding recliner.
- Soaking in a hot tub.

You can, however, buy a bit of assurance (but not *in*surance). One is the B&N Protection Plan, which replaces or repairs your NOOK if there's *accidental* damage (of the sort I just wrote about) two years from the day you bought it; it also extends the warranty against defects.

- The plan costs about 25 percent of the original purchase price.
- The plan *doesn't* protect you against mishaps that aren't accidental. If you admit to taking the NOOK into the shower or confess to microwaving it for science class, they're not going to laugh along with you.
- The plan *doesn't* cover a lost or stolen NOOK. To protect against that, get in touch with your insurance agent to see if you're protected under your homeowner's or renter's policy; some automobile policies also cover items that are stolen from a car.

Premium-level credit cards from American Express, MasterCard, and Visa generally offer added protection for devices that you've bought with those pieces of magic plastic. For example, they might offer 90-day theft coverage from the day of purchase. And some also add an extra year to the manufacturer's warranty against part failure. Contact customer service for any credit cards you own to see if this is included.

Resetting Your NOOK

If your NOOK becomes catatonic, you can perform a Vulcan mind meld — or as Barnes & Noble puts it, a *reset.* Resets come in two flavors. One is simple and benign (and can be done any time you'd like without concern). One is much more significant. Barnes & Noble customer support may tell you to perform a soft reset or a hard reset if your tablet is acting oddly or if the battery isn't properly recharging.

Soft reset

A *soft reset* tells the device to forget any recent commands or data. It doesn't erase any of your books, documents, or configuration settings. To soft reset, do this:

1. **Press and hold the power button for 20 seconds, then release the power button.**

   That's a fairly long time. About the length of most annoying television commercials for products you never knew you couldn't live without.

2. **Press the power button again for 3 seconds to turn on your tablet.**

Hard reset (Deregister)

Performing a hard reset is significant; it forces the NOOK Tablet to clears all temporary settings. It takes the tablet all the way back to factory default settings, and it erases all content: contacts, e-books, and more. You can restore anything you bought or downloaded from the NOOK Shop from the NOOK Cloud if you re-link the device to your B&N account. You have to reinstall anything you side loaded from a personal computer.

The only time you'll do a hard reset is when someone in customer service tells you to, or you want to erase your tablet before giving or reselling it to someone else.

To do a hard reset — wait, stop. Really? You sure?

1. **Tap the settings gear icon in the status bar.**

2. **Tap All Settings.**

3. **Tap Device Information in the category panel on the left.**

4. **Tap Erase & Deregister Device on the right.**

5. **Stop. Think. Think again. See Figure 7-3.**

6. **If you really, really want to do this, go to Step 7. If not, carefully tap somewhere outside of the menacing menu box.**

7. **Tap the Erase & Deregister Device button.**

Figure 7-3: Here is the way to completely clear your NOOK tablet's settings and content; this is an act of last resort.

Fixing Wireless Weirdness

Communication without wires means you're not likely to trip over them, lose them, damage them, or otherwise object to their presence. And just as importantly, wireless communication speaks to the very essence of portability of devices like a tablet. You can download a book or a file at home or at work, and move between those two places and tap into a Wi-Fi signal in an airport, train station, or coffee shop. I've been very few places in the world and unable to find a Wi-Fi signal to use with my tablet (and my smartphone and sometimes my laptop computer) to connect to the web.

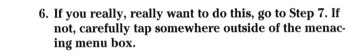

The NOOK HD or HD+ doesn't support voice over Internet services like Skype or Comwave, and Barnes & Noble has indicated it probably won't go there; it wants to concentrate on things related to reading and writing. Heads up, though: Microsoft has invested in Barnes & Noble, and Microsoft owns Skype, so future models could move in that direction.

If your wireless network isn't working properly, deal with that issue first. Here are some questions to ask:

- ✔ Is the Wi-Fi router powered up and connected to the Internet?
- ✔ Does the laptop or personal computer "see" and communicate with the adapter?
- ✔ Is the Internet service working? Check this from the computer.

Use your computer's troubleshooting tools to check its configuration. Plus, each wireless device has a built-in configuration and setup screen you can access from your computer. Here are some possible solutions:

- ✔ Turn off your NOOK and then turn it back on. Think of it as the equivalent of clearing your head by stepping outside into the cold morning.
- ✔ Turn off the power to the router for ten seconds or so and then restore power. That may fix a problem that has cropped up in the internal memory of the router.
- ✔ Check with the network administrator to see if there's a blacklist (of blocked devices) or a whitelist (of devices that are specifically allowed entrance) for the system if you're trying to connect to a secured system (at an office or somewhere similar). You may need to provide your NOOK tablet's MAC address (its unique identifier). To find the MAC address, go to Settings and tap Device Information.
- ✔ If all else fails, call Customer Service at 1-800-843-2665.

I see a wireless network but can't get a good connection

Wi-Fi networks cover a relatively small area (about the size of a small house). It may take a bit of experimentation to determine the actual working area for the Wi-Fi system you want to use.

- Go to Settings. In the Wireless section, look at the names of networks that the NOOK Tablet has discovered. Signal strength is shown to the right of each name: one to four stacked curves. Four curves means a strong signal. One curve means a weak signal, which may fade in and out.

- Take your tablet close to the Wi-Fi router or transmitter (7 feet away). Make sure no major pieces of metal are around to block the signal: refrigerators, file cabinets, or steel desks. (In some places, signals can be blocked by steel mesh in the walls.)

I see the network but I can't connect to it

Most wireless networks use a security system to keep unwanted outsiders from using them. You usually need a key or password, and some also require a username. You have to enter the key exactly. If the key is 6sJ7yEllowbIRD, then that is how you must enter it.

If your wireless system is at your home or office and you can't make it work with all of your devices, it might make sense to reset the Wi-Fi router to its factory default settings and reconfigure it with all of your devices ready to be connected. Consult the instruction manual for the Wi-Fi system to learn how to do this.

Updating the NOOK Operating System

The NOOK HD or HD+ software may change because B&N needs to fix problems or wants to add new features. In fact, the first users of the NOOK HD and HD+ (users like me) found an immediate update on the very first day the devices were available to the public.

In most cases, the updates automatically get put on the tablet when you connect over Wi-Fi. Updating the NOOK Tablet's software should take only a few minutes and doesn't affect your Library or your Keep Reading list, and an update doesn't change the device registration to your Barnes & Noble account.

There may be some situations where a major upgrade will require a different process (such as downloading a file to your personal computer and then bringing it across to the NOOK on the USB cable). Be sure to read and follow any instructions that appear on the screen of your reader or in email communications you may receive.

Don't Pay Twice, It's All Right

For people (like me) who travel a lot, one of the neatest things about the NOOK devices is the ability to read some of the same newspapers and magazines that are piling up on the desktop back home. But sometimes it makes you wonder why you're paying twice for the same material.

This is a problem that is still in the process of being solved, but some publishers have begun offering a discount on NOOK subscriptions to loyal customers who also have a subscription to the print version. Start by calling or emailing the publisher of the newspaper or magazine.

If they have seen the light and are offering a discount, it should be reflected at www.BN.com. However, you may have to do some work to introduce the bookstore to the publisher.

1. **Go to** www.BN.com **and visit My Account.**

2. **Locate the section called Manage Digital Subscriptions.**

   If the newspaper or magazine offers a discount and Barnes & Noble is aware of it, you should see a link to verify your print subscription information by entering your print subscription account number; that number is printed on the mailing label for the publication. If you have a discount but don't see it listed, call customer service and politely inquire about it.

Appy NOOK Day

The good news about the NOOK HD or HD+ is that it can learn new tricks when you download and install small special-purpose programs called *apps,* as in *applications.* The bad news is that most of them cost money. Many app developers let you test-drive their product in a free trial.

The smart news: If a developer offers a free trial, you should take advantage. It might take only a little bit to realize that the app is perfect for your needs; then you can pay the bill and have a copy of your very own. Or you might realize that it would be a waste of money to buy the app.

Look for a button labeled Free Trial as you browse the B&N app store. And be sure you understand the limitations.

- ✔ Some free trials give you full functionality, but only for a short period of time.

- ✔ Some free trials only give limited features.

- ✔ Some free trials let you experiment with the product but don't let you save or send anything you create using it.

If you accidentally somehow downloaded and paid for an app, get yourself quickly to a phone and call B&N Customer Service at 1-800-843-2665. They just may be able to uncharge your credit card.

Getting to the Root of It

The NOOK HD and HD+, as well as older cousins the NOOK Tablet and the NOOKcolor, share one important element in common: Their system software is based on the Android operating system. Android was developed by the globe-gobbling guys and gals of Google. (So, too, the Amazon Kindle Fire devices and many other tablets.)

The NOOK HD and HD+ run a modified version of Android version 4.0, also known by the seemingly sugar-addicted programmers at Google as Ice Cream Sandwich.

Apple keeps the iPad's iOS operating system locked under glass, but Google has been very open with its product, which is generally a good thing. However, every developer of hardware that uses Android is free to make modifications or add a restrictive outer shell on top of the operating system. That's the situation with Barnes & Noble, which keeps a tight grip on the system within its NOOK devices. If you follow all of their rules, you can only install apps that are approved by — and sold by — B&N. And you're also advised not to modify the operating system or replace it with another.

That said, technology is a continual game of cat and mouse. For whatever reason, dozens (if not thousands) of people dedicate uncounted hours to finding chinks in the armor so they can have their way with one or another of the NOOK tablets. The holy grail is the ability to *root* the system. This means finding a way to get at the deepest (or lowest) level of the operating system and make changes. Or the rooters may want to substitute a different version of Android with added features and no restriction on apps.

That's the place B&N would rather you not go, of course. I explain all of this because you deserve to know. For the record, I am *not* recommending that you attempt to root your system or otherwise adapt it to act in a way not endorsed by B&N.

Why? Because first of all, if you really want or need a tablet with features beyond the fairly complete set offered by Barnes & Noble, you can always buy a different device. Besides, B&N can — and has — made a number of updates to its NOOK tablets that have closed loopholes that hackers thought were open to them.

Getting to the root

By the time you read these words, I expect to see several offerings that will let you *root* or replace the NOOK operating system.

When someone *roots* a device, she can install apps that come from other sources (like Android Marketplace or directly from a programmer) and make other changes. The downside: B&N could update its operating system or refuse to honor warranty claims for a device that's been altered this way. (If you can use Erase & Deregister, that should remove all traces of rooting. Chapter 4 tells where to find that option.)

The rooters of rooting can be found looking online for **Cyanogenmod.**

Running a second operating system

You have an alternative to rooting. Instead of replacing the built-in Android operating system, you can put a special microSD card in the device and load a standard (non-NOOK) version of the Android operating system. In theory, this lets you expand some capabilities without deleting the B&N original code.

One company, N2A, expects to offer just such a *boot card* for the NOOK HD or HD+ by early 2013. It will allow use of an unmodified, more advanced version of the Android 4.1 system also known as Jelly Bean (sugar, anyone?). You can download the new OS and put it on your own microSD card for about $20, or buy a card with the OS installed for a bit more. You can find more details about the card at www.b2a.com.

If you choose to go this way, you can shop for apps and content at any store selling to Android marketplace.

Flashing Your NOOK

When the NOOK HD and HD+ were released, their web browser didn't support Adobe Flash Player. That was somewhat perturbing, and limiting, since many websites use Flash to show video.

I think it's quite likely that B&N will fix this shortcoming in an update to the operating system. But in the meantime, I found a way around the problem.

I used the web browser to visit a site that required use of Flash — the Amazon Prime page — and tried to watch a movie. A message said that I needed to install Flash to see the video; I told Amazon to go right ahead and put it in place. A few seconds later, Adobe Flash was installed and Amazon, YouTube, and other sites worked exactly as promised. I can't guarantee this will work for you, or that B&N won't break this fix, but go ahead and try: Select Flash for Android.

Index

• A •

accidental damage, 201
Account settings
  Adobe Digital Editions, 72
  UltraViolet, 71
ACSM files
  opening in Adobe Digital Editions, 157–158
  transferring, 157
Active Shelf
  defined, 25
  removing items from, 31
  settings, 61
Adobe Digital Editions
  downloading, 153
  installing, 153
  installing book files using, 153–154
  opening ACSM files in, 157–158
  preparing to use, 153
  settings, 72
Adobe Flash Player, 209
Adobe ID, 157
adult profile. *See also* profiles
  creating, 48–49
  defined, 48
  password protecting purchases for, 67
Advanced settings (web page)
  changing, 172–174
  illustrated, 173
  list of, 173–194
  locating, 173
Airplane Mode
  app, 199
  engaging, 199–200
  main control panel, 56
  switch, 55, 199
All Settings
  Account settings, 71–72
  Applications, 55–71
  defined, 55
  Device Information, 73–75
  General, 56–59
  Storage Management, 72–73
  Wireless & Bluetooth, 55–56
Amazon Prime video, 190
App button, 28
appearance (e-books), changing, 85
application settings
  Browser, 65–66
  Calendar, 63–64
  Contacts, 64–65
  Email, 62
  Home, 60–62
  Magazine/Catalog/Comics
    Reader, 66–67
  NOOK Video, 71
  Reader, 69–70
  Search, 70–71
  Shop, 67
  special accounts and NOOK
    Friends, 68–69
  working with, 59–71
apps
  browsing, 135
  buying (B&N Store), 126, 135–137
  defined, 183
  details, viewing, 136
  Email, 175–176
  free trial, 206–207
  Gallery, 196
  Hulu Plus, 189
  lack of, 134
  LendMe, 145
  on library shelves, 136
  Pandora, 186
  price display, 136
  purchasing, 112
  running, 137
  shelf illustration, 184
  supplied, 184–188

Apps tab, 29
archiving
  deleting versus, 142
  NOOK Cloud, 140–143
Article view (web browser), 166
attachments (email), 182
audio files. *See also* music player
  moving to NOOK, 186–187
  playing from Library, 187
  supported formats, 115

● *B* ●

B&N Top 100, 127
Barnes & Noble (B&N)
  gift cards, 134
  software, 121
Barnes & Noble (B&N) accounts
  creating, 121
  device registration to, 142–143
  linking to, 121
  refreshing to, 143
  syncing to, 143
Barnes & Noble (B&N) Store
  apps, 126, 134–137
  bill pay, 133–134
  book search, 127–128
  books, 124, 129–130
  catalogs, 126–127, 132–133
  kids, 125
  magazines, 124, 130–132
  movies & TV, 125
  newspapers, 126, 130–132
  offerings, 124–126
  shopping procedure, 124
  Top 100, 127
  WishList, 137–139
Barnes & Noble stores, taking
  NOOK to, 143
battery
  car charger, 198
  charger, 20
  charging checklist, 20–21
  charging steps, 21
  extending life of, 197–198

as fire risk, 197
high temperatures, avoiding, 197
hot, 197–198
information, 74
level, checking, 197
life, 197
life settings, 57
low charge alert, 197
new NOOK, 20
power adapter, 21
recharge time, 21
recharging, 198
status icon, 35
blacklist (blocked devices), 204
Bluetooth
  connectivity, 2
  defined, 162, 182
  device connection, 183
  functions, 182–183
  indicator, 34
  settings, 56
  sound quality, 183
book cover, press and hold, 40, 41
book design
  fonts, 99
  illustrated, 98, 100
  line spacing, 98
  margins, 99
  process, 97–100
  publisher defaults, 100
  size, 98
  themes, 99–100
bookmarks
  clearing, 94
  comic book, 107
  defined, 84–85
  reading page, 93
  scrapbook page, 97
  viewing, 93–94
  web browser, 165
Bookmarks tab, 29
books. *See* e-books
boot card, 209
borrowing books
  with LendMe, 148–149
  with Overdrive, 154–155

box, saving, 7
brightness settings, 55, 57–58
Browse mode (music player), 187–188
browser. *See* web browser
buying
  with Adobe Digital Editions, 152–154
  on Google e-bookstore, 157–158
  with Overdrive, 154–155
buying (B&N Store)
  billing address requirement, 118
  books, 129–130
  magazines, 130–132
  newspapers, 130–132
  from WishList, 139

• *C* •

Calendar, settings, 63–64
Calibre, 159
Camera (PTP) setting, 72
capacitive sensing, 9
car charger, 198
catalogs
  in B&N Store, 126
  buying from, 133
  flipping through, 108
  illustrated, 133
  subscribing to, 132–133
charging. *See also* battery
  checklist, 20–21
  not turning off while, 22
  steps, 21
child profile. *See also* profiles
  creating, 50–51
  defined, 50
  parental controls, 51, 52
  passcode, 52
children's books
  landscape mode, 103
  moving from page to page, 104
  Read and Play, 105–106
  Read and Record, 106–107
  reading, 103–107
  reading style, choosing, 105–107
  shopping for, 125
  skipping parts of, 104–105
  words and pictures, 105
cleaning touchscreen, 200
color graphics, 2
comic books, 107–108
computers
  ejecting NOOK from, 116–117
  moving files to NOOK from, 113–114
  troubleshooting tools, 204
contacts
  adding, 64, 146
  importing, 64
  listing, 147
  sharing quotes with, 91
Contacts app
  defined, 184
  settings, 64–65
cookies
  accepting, 172
  clearing, 172
  defined, 171
cool, keeping NOOK, 199
Customer Service, 204, 207
Customize Content Type setting, 62

• *D* •

daily inbox settings, 61
Date & Time settings, 59
dead NOOKs
  depleted battery and, 197
  recharger not working and, 198
  reenergizing, 196–198
deleting
  archiving versus, 142
  email, 181–182
  profiles, 53
desktop
  defined, 24
  panel indicators, 25
Developer Options setting, 75

Device Information settings
 defined, 73
 screen illustration, 74
 types of, 73–75
dictionary, 91–92
digital, defined, 193
Digital Rights Management (DRM),
 109, 152
double-tap, 40
Downloaded, book cover, 150
drag, 43
dry, keeping NOOK, 199

• *E* •

e-books. *See also* reading
 advanced navigation, 83–86
 Appearance icon, 85
 bookmarks, 84–85
 borrowing, 148–149
 buying in B&N Store, 124, 129–130
 Contents icon, 83
 covers, in Library, 150–151
 details page, 129
 downloading, 130
 EPUB, 109
 finding, 80
 highlights, 84
 installing with Adobe Digital
  Editions, 153–154
 jumping to pages, 82
 lending, 144–148
 navigating, 81–82
 notes, 84
 opening, 79–80
 page numbering, 80
 page slider, 81–82
 pages, turning, 80
 PDF, 109–110
 protected, 109
 samples, 129–130
 Search icon, 85
 searching for, 127–128

Share icon, 85, 86
 table of contents, 84
 unlocking, 152
 unprotected, 109
eGift cards, 134
ejecting NOOK, from computers,
 116–117
email
 addresses, 180
 attachments, 182
 deleting, 181–182
 forwarding, 181
 manager, opening, 28
 replying to, 181
 sending, 179–180
 settings, 62–63
 signature, changing, 180
 starting, 179
 subjects, 180
 typing, 179–180
 working with, 174–183
email accounts
 adding items from shortcuts
  to, 63
 with Email app, 175–176
 email provider information, 178
 IMAP, 177
 naming, 62
 POP, 177
 setting up manually, 177–178
 SMTP server, 178
Email app
 sending messages from, 180
 signature, changing, 180
 starting, 176
 using, 175–176
Email button, 28
Enable HotSpots setting, 67
EPUBs, 109, 111
Erase & Deregister Device
 setting, 75
e-reader functions, 2
Excel files, 111

• F •

Facebook
  posting LendMe offer on, 147–148
  settings, 68–69
  sharing quotes and, 91
Feedbooks, 159
files
  audio, 186–187
  backup copies, 113
  moving from computer to NOOK, 113–114
  preparing for NOOK, 114–115
  side loading, 110
  supported formats, 115–116
  types of, 111–112
  videos, 188–189
Find in Book feature, 92–93
Flash for Android, 209
flash memory. *See* microSD cards
folders, 114
fonts, in book design, 99
form data, filling, 172
formatting
  defined, 19
  SD cards, 19–20
forwarding email, 182
free trials
  apps, 206–207
  magazines, 130, 132
  newspapers, 130, 132
friends
  inviting, 144–145
  lending books of, 146–148
  lending books to, 145–146
  in LendMe program, 144

• G •

Gallery
  defined, 185
  viewing screenshots with, 196

General settings, 56–59
gestures
  double-tap, 40
  drag, 43
  lift, 43
  notes, 88–90
  pinch, 43–44, 107
  press, 44
  press and hold, 40–41
  reading, 78
  scroll, 42
  swipe, 41–42
  tap, 39
gift cards, 134
Gift Cards setting, 67
Gmail, 174, 175
Google accounts, 157
Google e-bookstore
  ACSM file transfer, 157
  buying on, 157–158
  illustrated, 156
  reading public domain books via, 156–157
  using, 155–158
Google Play, 155
Gutenberg Project, 109

• H •

hard reset
  as action of last resort, 202
  defined, 202
  process, 203
highlights
  adding, 87–88
  color, changing, 90
  expanding, 88
  removing, 90
Home button
  functions, 10
  identification, 10
  illustrated, 8, 9
  in unlocking tablet, 22

Home screen
  Active Shelf, 25
  adding items from shortcuts to, 31–32
  changing, 30–32
  desktop, 24, 25
  elements of, 23–24
  illustrated, 24
  nav buttons, 25–28
  orientation to, 30–31
  removing items from, 32
  Search tool, 35–36
  shortcuts menu, 28–29
  status bar, 25
  system bar, 25, 35–36
  using, 24–30
Home settings
  Customize Content Types, 62
  Quick Corner Action, 60–61
  Select Shelf Behavior, 61
  Show Issues of Subscriptions, 62
Hulu Plus. *See also* videos
  app, 189
  app future, 185
  defined, 185
  subscribing to, 189
  use requirements, 188

• *I* •

icons, this book, 4
images
  processing for NOOK, 115
  reading capability, 112
  supported formats, 115
IMAP email accounts, 177
in-plane switching (IPS), 9
InStore network, 143
international travel, with NOOK, 118

• *J* •

JavaScript, enabling, 174

• *K* •

Keyboard setting, 58

• *L* •

Language setting, 58
Legal information, 75
lending books
  friend invitations and, 144–145
  to NOOK friends, 145–146
  of NOOK friends, 146–149
LendMe
  app, 145
  badge, 145
  book cover, 151
  defined, 144
  to find lendable books, 148–149
  offer, sending, 68, 146, 147
  offer acceptance, 68, 148
  terms and conditions, 148
  use requirement, 69
Lent, book cover, 151
Library
  book covers, 150–151
  defined, 26
  managing, 150–152
  navigating, 27–28
  playing audio files from, 187
  Privacy Settings, 149–150
  Search tool, 36
  shelves, building, 151–152
  shelves illustration, 26
  standard shelves, 27
  system bar, 36
Library tab, 29
lift, 43
line spacing, in book design, 98
loaning books, 146–148
Lock Rotation, 55, 57
locking, 22
long press. *See* press and hold
lossless compressed files, 195

• M •

Macintosh computers/laptops,
  ejecting NOOK from, 117
magazines
  Article view, 102
  buying in B&N Store, 124, 130–132
  buying single issue, 130–132
  content navigation, 102
  international travel and, 118
  Page view, 101
  print subscriptions and, 206
  reading, 100–102
  searching for, 128
  subscribing to, 132
  trials, 130, 132
  unlocking, 152
Manage Credit Card setting, 67, 68
Manybooks.net, 159
margins, in book design, 99
Media device (MTP) setting, 72
messages (email)
  attachments, 182
  deleting, 181–182
  forwarding, 181
  replying to, 181
  sending, 179–180
  starting, 179
  subjects, 180
  typing, 179–180
microSD cards
  Class 6 speed, 16
  defined, 12
  as flash memory, 15
  formatting, 19–20
  holding, 17
  illustrated, 16
  inserting, 19
  installing, 17–19
  manufacturer, 16
  removing, 18
  specs recommendation, 16
  types of, 15
  unformatted, 19

microSD slot
  defined, 12
  opening cover, 18
Microsoft Office documents, 115
microsUSB, 21
Model Number, 74
movies. *See* NOOK Video
music files
  reading capability, 111
  supported formats, 115
music player
  Browse mode, 187–188
  defined, 185
  modes, 187–188
  moving audio files to, 186–187
  Now Playing mode, 188
  playing audio files from, 187
  press and hold, 41

• N •

nav buttons
  App, 28
  defined, 25
  Email, 28
  Library, 26
  location of, 25–26
  Shop, 28
  types of, 26
  Web, 28
navigation
  e-book, 83–86
  magazine, 102
Netflix, 189
New, book cover, 150
newspapers
  buying in B&N Store, 126
  buying single issue, 130–132
  opening, 103
  print subscriptions and, 206
  reading, 102–103
  subscribing to, 132
  trials, 130, 132
  unlocking, 152

NOOK
  back, 13–15
  bottom, 11–12
  dead, reenergizing, 196–198
  defined, 1
  ejecting from computer, 116–117
  features, 1–3
  front, 8–10
  keeping dry and cool, 199
  left side, 12–13
  limitations, 3
  locking/unlocking, 22
  model comparison, 6
  models, 5
  moving files from computer to,
    113–114
  preparing files for, 114–115
  registering, 120–122
  resetting, 202–203
  right side, 13
  as storage device, 11
  top side, 10–11
  traveling abroad with, 118
  turning off, 13
  uses, 6–7
  warranty, improving, 201–202
NOOK Cloud
  archiving, 140–143
  defined, 140
  deleting versus archiving and, 142
  getting items from, 141
  items types in, 140
  moving items to, 141
  not included in, 141
  restoring from, 140
  storage, viewing, 141–142
  syncing with, 140
NOOK Friends
  adding, 144–145
  defined, 185
  lending books to, 145–146
  network, 144
  Privacy Settings, 149–150
NOOK HD
  back panel, 13, 15
  external parts illustration, 9

folders, 114
internal storage, 72
left side, 12–13
NOOK HD+ comparison, 6
power button, 44
processing images for, 115
resolution, 1
right side, 13
top side, 10–11
turning on/off, 12
volume buttons, 44
NOOK HD+
  back panel, 13–14
  buttons, ports, slots, 8
  folders, 114
  NOOK HD comparison, 6
  power button, 44
  processing images for, 115
  resolution, 1
  right side, 13
  top side, 11
  volume buttons, 44
NOOK notch, 10
NOOK Shop. *See also* Barnes &
    Noble (B&N) Store
  apps, 126, 134–136
  bill pay, 133–134
  book search, 127–128
  books, 124, 129–130
  catalogs, 126–127
  kids, 125
  magazines, 124, 130–132
  movies & TV, 125
  newspapers, 126, 130–132
  sections, 124–127
  settings, 67–68
  system bar, 37–38
  WishList, 137–139
NOOK symbol, 10
NOOK Today
  illustrated, 30
  interface, 29–30
  newsletter, reading, 29
NOOK Video. *See also* videos
  backup, 191
  content, 190

illustrated, 126
settings, 71
streaming option, 125
as work in progress, 190–191
notes
  adding, 88–90
  adding to scrapbook pages, 96
  editing, 89
  gestures, 88–90
  removing, 89
  searching, 88
  viewing, 89
  viewing on scrapbook pages, 96
notifications
  area (status bar), 33–34
  settings, 59
Now Playing mode (music player),
  188

• *O* •

OfficeSuite, 116
online calendars, 63
operating system
  Android, 207
  changing, 137
  second, running, 209
  updating, 205–206
Overdrive
  defined, 154
  illustrated, 155
  obtaining, 154
  using, 154–155

• *P* •

page slider
  defined, 81
  Go to Page button, 82
  moving forward/backward with, 82
  using, 81–82
Page Turn setting, 67
pages
  bookmarking, 93–94
  going to, 82

numbering of, 80
printed versions versus
  electronic, 80
scrapbook, 94–97
turning, 80
Pandora app, 186
panel indicators, 25
parental controls, 51, 52
passwords
  best, 123
  child profile, 52
  clearing, 172
  as first line of defense, 170
  for purchases, 123–124
  reasons for creating, 122
  removing, 123
  requirement benefit, 124
  web settings, 172
PDF e-books, 109–110, 111
periodicals. *See* magazines;
  newspapers
Personal Dictionary setting, 58
pinch, 43–44
plug adapter, 22
plug-ins, enabling, 174
png files, screenshots, 195
Pointer Speed setting, 58
POP email accounts, 177
Popular Lists, 127
pop-ups, blocking, 174
power
  battery, 20–21
  from wall, 21–22
power adapter
  connecting to plug adapter, 22
  defined, 21
  illustrated, 21
PowerPoint files, 111
Pre-order, book cover, 150
press, 43–44
press and hold
  defined, 40
  screen variations, 40–41
primary profile, 48
print periodical subscriptions,
  206

privacy settings
  configuring, 170–172
  cookies, 171–172
  critical, 171
  form data, 172
  illustrated, 170
  locating, 171
Privacy Settings (NOOK Friends), 149–150
profiles
  adult, 48–50
  changing, 53
  child, 50–52
  deleting, 53
  editable, icons of, 53
  number of, 49
  primary, 48
  support, 47
  types of, 47
Project Gutenberg, 159
protected books, 109
publication formats, 108–110
publisher defaults, in book design, 100

• *Q* •

Quick Corner Action settings, 60–61
Quick Settings panel
  accessing, 34–35
  Airplane Mode, 55
  All Settings, 55
  Brightness, 55
  defined, 55–59
  Home settings, 54
  illustrated, 54
  Lock Rotation, 55
  using, 54–55
  Wi-Fi, 55
QWERTY keyboard layout, 44–45

• *R* •

Read and Play books, 105–106
Read and Record books, 106–107
Reader
  defined, 69
  settings, 69–71
reader assumptions, this book, 3
reading. *See also* e-books
  catalogs, 108
  children's books, 103–107
  comic books, 107–108
  as easy, 7
  e-books, 78–100
  gestures, 78, 83
  magazines, 100–102
  newspapers, 102
  publication formats, 108–110
  secondary tools, 86–93
  tools, 83
Recent Drawer
  Library system bar, 36
  Shop system bar, 38
  using, 38
Recent Read, 38–39, 61
recent reading
  Library system bar, 36
  returning to, 38–39
  Shop system bar, 38
Recents icon, 37
recharger, 198
Recommended, book cover, 150
recording
  ending, 107
  listening to, 106
  playing, 107
  rerecording, 107
  tips, 106–107
refreshing NOOK, to B&N account, 143
registration (NOOK)
  steps for, 120–121
  Wi-Fi connection for, 120

replying to email, 182
resets
  defined, 202
  hard, 202–203
  soft, 202
resolution
  comparison, 1
  feature, 2
rooting
  defined, 207
  downside, 208

● *S* ●

samples
  in Barnes & Noble stores, 143
  book cover, 150
  e-book, 129–130
scrapbooks
  adding notes to, 96
  bookmarks, 97
  clipping pages for, 94–97
  creating, 95
  moving through, 97
  removing pages from, 97
  saving pages in, 95
  viewing, 96
  viewing notes in, 96
screen captures
  button press for, 194
  defined, 194
  getting off NOOK, 195
  making, 194–196
  numbering, 196
  as png files, 195
  viewing, 194
  viewing with Gallery app, 196
Screen Timeout setting, 58
scroll, 42
Search tool, 35–36, 37
searches
  e-book, 85, 92–93, 128
  note, 88

periodical, 128
settings for, 70–71
second operating system, running,
  209
secondary reading tools
  defined, 86
  dictionary, 91–92
  displaying, 86
  Find in Book feature, 92–93
  highlight, 87–88
  notes, 88–90
  Share Quote feature, 90–91
  types of, 87
secure digital (SD) cards, 15
security settings
  critical, 171
  General settings, 59
  locating, 171
  passwords, 172
  Select Shelf Behavior settings, 61
Serial Number, 74
Server Settings screen, 177
setting up
  all settings, 55–59
  application settings, 59–71
  profiles, 47–53
  with Quick Settings panel, 54
Share Quote feature, 90–91
sharing
  e-books, 85, 86
  quotes, 90–91
shelves. *See also* Library
  adding items to, 151–152
  app, 184
  building, 151–152
  illustrated, 26
  navigating, 27–28
  standard, 27
Shop button, 28
shortcuts menu
  adding items to Home screen
    from, 31–32
  defined, 28–29

shortcuts menu *(continued)*
  tabs, 29
  viewing, 29
side loading files
  with Adobe Digital Editions,
    153–154
  defined, 110
  file types, 111–112
  with USB cable, 110–111
  videos, 188
signature, changing, 180
Skype, 203, 204
sleep
  waking up from, 22
  Wi-Fi radio and, 13
SMTP server, 178
soft reset, 202
Software Version, 74
sound settings, 58
status bar
  battery status, 35
  Bluetooth indicator, 34
  center part, 33–34
  checking, 32–35
  defined, 25
  displaying, 33
  illustrated, 33
  left part, 33
  notifications area, 33–34
  Quick Settings panel, 34–35
  right part, 34–35
  time, 34
  user name, 33
  Wi-Fi indicator, 34
storage management settings,
    72–73
subscriptions
  print magazine and newspaper,
    206
  settings, 62
supplied apps
  Contacts, 184
  Gallery, 185
  Hulu Plus, 185
  music player, 185, 186–188

NOOK Friends, 185
types of, 184–186
swipe. *See also* gestures
  defined, 41
  illustrated, 42
  use examples, 41
syncing, 143
system bar
  defined, 25, 35
  Home screen, 35–36
  illustrated, 35
  Library, 36
  Shop, 37–38

● *T* ●

table of contents, 84
tap, 39
terms of service, 121
text files, 111
Text-to-Speech Output setting, 58
themes, in book design, 99–100
30-pin connector
  defined, 11
  look-a-like connectors versus, 12
  purposes, 11
  USB cable, 21
touchscreen
  capacitive sensing, 9
  cleaning, 200
  viewing angles, 9
traveling abroad, 118
trials. *See* free trials
TV. *See* NOOK Video
Twitter, sharing quotes and, 91
typing on NOOK, 7

● *U* ●

UltraViolet
  settings, 71
  technology, 191
unlocking, 22
unprotected books, 109